The Library of World Biography

VII · VI · LXII
in Vaticano

Pope John XXIII

by Paul Johnson

THE LIBRARY OF WORLD BIOGRAPHY

J. H. PLUMB, GENERAL EDITOR

Little, Brown and Company — Boston – Toronto

FIRST EDITION

T 11/74

LIBRARY OF CONGRESS CATALOGING IN PUBLICATION DATA

Johnson, Paul, 1928–
    Pope John XXIII.

    (Library of world biography)
    Bibliography: p.
    1. Joannes XXIII, Pope, 1881–1963. I. Title.
BX1378.2.J66   263'.13'0924 [B]   74-12325
ISBN 0-316-467553

*Published simultaneously in Canada
by Little, Brown & Company (Canada) Limited*

PRINTED IN THE UNITED STATES OF AMERICA

This book is dedicated
by permission
to another wise and energetic pastor
the Reverend Patrick L. Grady
of Eskadale Mission Church, Inverness-shire

Certainly, it is heaven upon earth, to have a man's mind move in charity, rest in Providence, and turn upon the poles of truth.

— FRANCIS BACON
Essay on Truth

Introduction

WHEN WE LOOK BACK at the past nothing, perhaps, fascinates us so much as the fate of individual men and women. The greatest of these seem to give a new direction to history, to mold the social forces of their time and create a new image, or open up vistas that humbler men and women never imagined. An investigation of the interplay of human temperament with social and cultural forces is one of the most complex yet beguiling studies a historian can make; men molded by time, and time molded by men. It would seem that to achieve greatness both the temperament and the moment must fit like a key into a complex lock. Or rather a master key, for the very greatest of men and women resonate in ages distant to their own. Later generations may make new images of them — one has only to think what succeeding generations of Frenchmen have made of Napoleon, or Americans of Benjamin Franklin — but this only happens because some men change the course of history and stain it with their own ambitions, desires, creations or hopes of a magnitude that embraces future generations like a miasma. This is particularly true of the great figures of religion, of politics, of war. The great creative spirits, however, are used by subsequent generations in a reverse manner — men and women go to them to seek hope or solace, or to confirm despair, reinterpreting the works of imagination or wisdom to ease them in their own desperate necessities, to beguile them with a sense of beauty or merely to draw from them strength and understanding. So this series of biographies tries, in lucid, vivid, and dramatic narratives, to explain the greatness of men and women, not only how they managed to secure their niche in the great pantheon of Time, but also why they have continued to fascinate subsequent generations. It may seem, therefore, that it is paradoxical for this series to contain living men and women, as well as the dead, but it is not so. We can recognize, in our own time, particularly in those whose careers are getting close to their final hours, men and women of indisputable greatness, whose position in history is secure, and about whom the legends and myths are beginning to sprout — for all great men and women become legends, all become in history larger than their own lives.

It is rare to achieve greatness in old age, but that is exactly what Pope John XXIII achieved. When Pius XII died, there was scarcely any institution in the world, save the Japanese monarchy or the Dalai Llama of Tibet's government, which had adjusted less to the modern world.

Other churches had searched their souls about over-population and family planning, the position of women in society, racism and class, the maldistribution of food, the desirability of de-institutionalizing religion, or at least making the ritual easier to comprehend. Certainly there had been a gentle and hesitant movement towards a less rigid conservatism within the church itself, but progress had been fitful, usually negligible, and mostly confined to a diocese and a bishop. The citadel of the Curia in Rome seemed as adamantine in its strength, as certain of its power and authority, as it had been in the 1880s. But there were currents of unease within the laity of the church, and there were priests and bishops, and an occasional cardinal, who responded cautiously to the sense of disquiet. Many had been troubled by the church's intransigent political conservatism. Even by the most sympathetic interpretation of Pius XII's policy to Hitler and to Mussolini, it could only be interpreted as negative. There was no thunderous denunciation of the violation of the sanctities of human life from the throne of Saint Peter. Such actions might have led the pope to calvary, and the church to a terrible destruction, but, at least, the deepest principles of Catholic Christianity — the sanctity of all human life — would have been vindicated. Nor was the Curia's attitude to social justice any more impressive. Regimes of acknowledged brutality that condemned the majority of their citizens to grinding poverty and its concomitant evils were accepted, and often tacitly and sometimes openly blessed. The Blacks in America, initially, found no champions in the Catholic hierarchy. But there were priests in South America sensitive to the conditions of life in the slums of Rio, São Paulo, Caracas, or in the sad villages of the Andean highlands. There were plenty of laymen and laywomen of compassionate social consciousness. And there were a number of high-minded, ambitious politiques in the corridors of the Vatican, or secure in the confidence of a prelate or cardinal, who felt that total intransigence towards the Communist powers of Eastern Europe could only be disastrous for those Catholics, and there were millions of them, who lived beyond the Iron Curtain. All of these seismic rumblings scarcely echoed in the Vatican itself, when audiences and medals and niceties of ritual ate up the days. And the administrators of the church were more worried by the pope's housekeeper or his visions in the garden than the social disasters which threatened mankind. When, at last, Pius XII died, there was no sense of crisis, no sharp division between progressives and reactionaries, and the election of the aged patriarch of Venice seemed unlikely to herald a new era in the history of the church.

That happened. John XXIII was not, or he would never have been elected pope, a dedicated liberal with a coherent vision of what a renewed Catholic church should be in the modern world. In many ways he was deeply traditional, possessing an old-fashioned piety for particular saints, their days, their churches, their acts and sayings and devotions. Yet his character was as complex as his compassion was deep. Knowing that time might be short, he acted with speed. He summoned the first General Council of the church since 1870, and began to push the Curia from its hieratic isolation back into the turmoil of the world. Above all, he set an intensely human example of goodness — living and acting with simplicity — always approachable, never remote. In four dramatic years the forces of liberation were locked in combat with the traditional attitudes of the Curia; among the Catholic laity itself new and powerful voices were unleashed. Some bishops acted with astounding independence, at least in the light of the past. The church can never be the same again after Pope John XXIII, any more than it was after Gregory the Great or Hildebrand. A man of hope who never feared reality, he unleashed forces that are still foaming in turbulence.

— J. H. PLUMB

Contents

Pope John XXIII

ONE

Rules of Life

WRITING THE LIFE OF A POPE is not an easy task. A man comes to the throne of Saint Peter at an age when most public officials are seeking retirement. He is brought from comparative obscurity to startling world prominence, and his previous career, which usually embraces most of his working life, is quickly embellished with pious anecdotes and edifying inventions. The Roman Catholic church, in its higher reaches, is a secretive organization, and the Vatican itself is an authoritarian court and government which repulses inquirers and protects its sovereign behind a wall of protocol. Its state papers are published, if at all, only after the lapse of many years, and sometimes vital elements of the truth do not emerge for generations. Then, too, the pope asserts the supernatural power of divine guidance in the central aspect of his ministry, the illumination of faith and morals. It is not always clear to the historian when his policies are shaped by his own judgment, and when they are directed by the relationship he claims with Providential forces; his reign thus defies normal political analysis. His actions have to be seen not merely in their contemporary context but *sub specie aeternitatis*; he directs a global organization whose temporal functions are often in conflict with its deeper spiritual purposes, and whose successes or failures cannot be identified by the criteria of secular society. What constitutes a good pope is very much a subjective matter.

The life of John XXIII raises particular problems. He was nearly seventy-seven when he was elected, after an undistinguished career which is ill-documented, at least in terms of papers open to public inspection. His impact on his times, and therefore his interest to us, was confined to the last four and a half years of his life. It was considerable, indeed unprecedented in this century; but for this very reason it has attracted mythologists and mystery-makers. Some of his partisans have invested him with quasi-miraculous powers of perception; his critics, on the other hand, have systematically undervalued his deliberative intellect, and present his pontificate as a series of uncontrolled accidents. The radiance of his character appeals to millions, but the strength of the public *persona* he so rapidly acquired has to some extent concealed his inner motivation and his true nature.

But despite these handicaps, a study of Pope John offers impressive rewards to the biographer. He was neither a simple nor an unsophisticated man; but there was no real mystery about him either. There was a unity about his life, work and character which allows one to present a clear and faithful portrait, and which provides satisfying

explanations for all he said and did. There was no dichot-
omy between his private life and his public acts. Granted
his spiritual assumptions, which were formed early in life
and tenaciously held until the end, his pontificate was
wholly consistent with his earlier career, indeed adumbrated by it. His fascination as a public person lies in his
efforts to apply strictly spiritual principles to the solution
of temporal problems. But beyond this, though directly
related to it, was his lifelong personal struggle to acquire
goodness, and so to save his soul. He is thus of equal interest both to students of human wisdom and students of
moral philosophy; and his magnetism transcends intellectual categories. Pope John illustrates the continuing power
of moral forces to influence events. In that sense, his life
is truly edifying.

Angelo Giuseppe Roncalli was born in Sotto il Monte
on 25 November 1881. The place can be termed a north
Italian mountain village, though in fact it lies on the very
edge of the great Lombardy plain. It is grouped along the
first high ridge east of Lake Como, the foothills of the
massive Bergamesque mountains which rise to the north.
Bergamo is six miles away to the east, and Sotto is just
inside the frontier which demarcated the ancient Republic of Venice from the Duchy of Milan. The Bergamese
are independent-minded and strongly attached to their
traditions of freedom. Their adherence to the Republic
was voluntary, and indeed Bergamo provided one of its
most distinguished military commanders, the *condottiere*
Bartolomeo Colleoni. His splendid equestrian statue is
in Venice, but his body rests in its own Renaissance chapel

in the ancient Bergamo church of Santa Maria Maggiore. The Bergamese hated the Austrian tyranny, and provided the largest single contingent, 170 men, in Garibaldi's liberating "thousand." But their patriotism was, and is, provincial rather than national. It is curious that Roncalli never read Mazzini until he was already over eighty. He often asserted that he was a good Italian; but his affections were anchored in his region. He was Bergamesque to his bones. He liked its landscape, its food, its wit and irony, its songs, its decorative arts. Donizetti, who is buried in Bergamo, was among his favorite composers; and it was another Bergamesque, Manzu, who he employed to cast the new bronze door of Saint Peter's. No pope was more conscientiously opposed to nepotism than John XXIII; but when he felt he could legitimately exercise favor, it was clergy from Bergamo who were singled out. When he looked for wider horizons, he turned to Venice, the old protectress of his province. Roncalli was by instinct a regionalist; and this provided the basis for his subsequent convictions as an internationalist. The point is an important one. He was singularly immune to the violent nationalist emotions which inflicted such destruction in his lifetime: he moved easily and logically from the natural affections of a regional son to the broader concept of a world society in which all peoples, as he preached, had a God-given right to maintain their traditional cultures and exercise their local freedoms. With his strong sense of history, he saw the Bergamesques as a once-oppressed people, and this gave him a powerful affinity with subject races throughout the world, and a well-reasoned dislike for the exercise of state power to enforce the more extravagant claims of nationality.

Within the provincial structure lay the family unit, itself part of the larger village organism. Roncalli believed that his family first came to Sotto about 1500, settling in the higher part of the village called Camaitino or the House of Martin, after a Martin Roncalli. Frescoes on the old house include a coat of arms, a tower on a field of red and white bars, which Roncalli adopted as his crest when he was made a bishop. Roncalli had a deep regard for family history, and for the subsection of the village where his forebears had lived. The old church at Camaitino became ruinous in his lifetime, and the family went to the lower village, Brusico, to worship at the church of Santa Maria. But after the First World War, Roncalli organized the building of a new church at Camaitino, which he himself consecrated in 1929; and for many years he rented a little holiday-house nearby, where his two surviving sisters remained until their deaths in the 1950s. His family and village *pietas* was expressed after his election as pope, when he chose the name John, as he explained, after his father and the old church of San Giovanni in the upper hamlet. Roncalli's local and family origins were humble; but they were, nonetheless, rooted and secure. His confidence in belonging contributed to the serenity which was so marked a characteristic of his mature personality.

The Roncallis were prolific and long-lived. Angelo had twelve brothers and sisters, ten of whom survived childhood. He had three elder sisters, who gave him their affection, and to one of whom he remained deeply attached.

His grandfather lived to be eighty-eight, his great-uncle to eighty-eight, his father to eighty-one, his mother to eighty-five. They were, and had been for centuries, tenant farmers, or *mezzadri,* renting their land from the local squire, Count Morlani. Roncalli used to joke: "There are three ways of ruining yourself — wine, women and agriculture. My father chose the dullest." When Angelo was born, the family shared a primitive house-and-stable with ten cousins. It was built round a small farmyard, the kitchen and mangers on the ground floor, the bedrooms above reached by an outside staircase. But the family was rising above subsistence poverty. In 1891, when Angelo was nine, they took over a much bigger house, La Colombera, which had eighteen rooms; and nearly thirty years later his father and brothers were able to buy their land from the Count. Roncalli later recorded: "There was never any wheat-bread on our table, only *polenta* [maize]. No wine for the children and young people, and rarely meat. Only at Christmas and Easter did we have a slice of home-made cake." The atmosphere was austere, puritanical and pietistic. His great-uncle, Zaverio Roncalli, led the family in reciting the rosary every evening, and read extracts from the homilies of the Spanish Jesuit Luis da Ponte. As the cleverest of the children, Angelo was quickly and automatically oriented towards the priesthood — then virtually the only means by which a boy of his class could hope to rise in the world.

Angelo's childhood was secure, even hopeful; but it was not easy, and in some ways it became progressively more difficult. After he was confirmed at the age of seven, a local priest began to teach him Latin, from Caesar's *De*

Bello Gallico. He was conscientious but not brilliant, and he was much beaten. There was nothing in his family background to assist a peasant-scholar. At the age of nine he was sent to the nearest diocesan seminary at Celana, walking there and back once a week. He was unhappy and unsuccessful, and the experiment was ended after two terms. Then, in 1892, their landlord's brother, Canon Morlani of Bergamo Cathedral, got him a boarder's place in the town seminary, where he slowly established a reputation for diligence and good conduct. In June 1895, at the age of thirteen, he received the tonsure, and from this point we begin to know something about him, for he marked the event by opening a spiritual diary, published after his death under the title of *Giornale dell'Anima.**

This work has led to some misapprehension about the nature of Roncalli's character and spirituality. Its publication, in fact, disturbed many progressive Catholics, who had much admired his pontificate, for it seemed to reflect a quite exceptionally simple, even naive, approach to the religious life. It is always possible to fall into a fundamental error by isolating certain aspects of Roncalli's devotions. Thus, after his death, Dr. John Heenan, cardinal-archbishop of Westminster, wrote in his *Cathedral Chronicle* for July 1964: "I doubt if he had read many of the books of contemporary theologians. He made scholars smile when he told them the name of his favourite bed-side book — Father Faber's *All for Jesus.*" He was, said Dr. Heenan, a "pastoral pope with his childlike devotions . . . the old-fashioned 'Garden of the Soul' type of Catholic. . . . He was not an original thinker. It was Pope Pius

---

* In English translation, *Journal of a Soul.*

XII, not Pope John, who allowed married pastors to become priests, revised the rules for the Eucharistic fast, and introduced evening mass. Pope John was no innovator. He was responsible for no great reform."

This view tends to be confirmed by a cursory reading of the diary. Roncalli began it on the instructions of his superiors. It was not a private document but a training exercise, to be periodically produced for inspection and comment. It opens with a passage termed "The Rules of Life," a routine seminarians' text, which Roncalli was told to copy out. There is some evidence that his guides deprecated the intrusion of personal details and thoughts, and told the youth to make it less of a diary and more of an exercise in self-discipline and pietism. Though Bergamo was undoubtedly a progressive town by the standards of late-nineteenth-century Italian Catholicism, the seminary was exceptionally strict, and Roncalli's spiritual and academic training was conducted on very narrow lines. At home, he had access to two newspapers, the Catholic daily, *L'Eco di Bergamo,* and a similar weekly, *Il Campanone.* At the seminary, newspapers of any kind were forbidden, nor were the students encouraged, or even allowed, to hold discussions which had no direct bearing on their training. Much of what Roncalli wrote reflects simply the views of his mentors. The wonder is, in the circumstances, that some elements of his own personality survive — and these are of considerable interest.

The main object of the diary was to identify his moral failings, and to record his progress in eliminating them. Most of his "sins" appear pretty humdrum: gossiping in the kitchen at home, drowsing during meditations, taking too long a siesta, eating too much fruit, failing to wear his heavy clerical clothes while out walking — the natural failings of a jovial, extrovert youth with a tendency to put on too much weight. Sex, as he later recalled, did not worry him very much, an impression confirmed by the diary, though he went through the usual exercises: "I shall be careful to mortify my feelings severely, keeping them within the limits of Christian modesty; especially shall I discipline my eyes, which St. Ambrose called insidious snares, and St. Anthony of Padua thieves of the soul. . . . With women of any kind, be they even relatives or saintly, I shall be especially careful, fleeing from their friendship, their companionship or their conversation, especially if they are young; nor will I ever look them in the face . . . Never will I confide in them at all, and when I needs must speak with them I will be careful to use speech that is firm, brief, prudent and upright." This is a boy of sixteen, repeating by rote the precepts of his spiritual adviser. In preparing for a life of clerical celibacy, it is necessary to acquire certain patterns of behavior which soon become instinctive and cease to be irksome. Roncalli seems to have taken to them easily, without acquiring the ingrained suspicion of women characteristic of many celibates; his relationships with women throughout his mature life were open, friendly, unselfconscious and entirely innocent.

What did concern him, and rightly, were the problems of pride and obedience, and it is his struggles with these which give the diary its intrinsic interest and cast valuable light on the man. Roncalli was the clever son of poor rustics, clearly destined to rise above their station, and possibly to become a prince of the church. His admission to the Bergamo seminary was marked by the privilege of a separate room in their house, and during term-time he lived a life quite remote from theirs. It was in the holidays that he became quickly conscious of a gap between his life and his family's — a gap marked by different standards of cleanliness, comfort, speech, manners, attitudes and interests, and one certain to become unbridgeable. Roncalli later accused himself of snobbery. His cousins complained, through the parish priest, who passed it on to the seminary, that he "gave himself airs." On his first vacation, a Franciscan friar lodged a further complaint, which he noted on 3 June 1898: "My superiors have received an account, I think exaggerated, of my having behaved arrogantly during the vacation, and I have been duly rebuked . . . it has been a nasty blow, and has given me food for thought and tears . . . pride is always present and it is this pride which gave rise to accusations." He found living with his family a constant trial: "Only three days of the vacation have passed, and already I am weary with them. At the sight of so much unhappiness, in the midst of such mistrust, oppressed by so many fears, often I sigh, sometimes I weep." He writes again of "those cursed holidays." Aged seventeen, he notes: ". . . as for the trials of family life, renewed especially during the vacation, I have offered them all up to the blessed heart of Jesus." His family were preoccupied with the grim struggle for existence, the harsh peasant's need to sell crops and beasts for cash; they quarreled among themselves about money and work. His worries, and interests, were quite different. He told himself he must not get into discussions with them after supper: "They certainly have their worries, and many of them! But my own are of a different kind. Theirs are about their bodies and material things; mine are about souls." At eighteen he was greatly distressed by a quarrel with his mother: he had rebuked her for expressing curiosity about "a certain matter." In a sense he was already their social superior, indeed moral mentor. It was a difficult role to thrust on a warm-hearted, extrovert adolescent. He was conscious that he had to hold himself apart from their grinding obsessions with money; but conscious, also, that they had made sacrifices to raise him in life, and might reasonably expect some sort of return. Nevertheless, he had to make it plain that they would get nothing from any success he enjoyed in his clerical career: "What profit would it be to possess all the gold in the world if one were to lose one's soul? Keep this truth in mind and never forget it." He made his intentions clear, and stuck to them: no poor family ever benefited less from the rise of an able offspring. A photograph taken in Rome in March 1925, when Roncalli was consecrated bishop, makes the point with cruel exactness: the new bishop sits in the front row, surrounded by plump clerics and well-dressed secular bigwigs; his aged parents, his brothers and sisters, stand humbly behind. Roncalli knew that the way in which successful clerics helped their families was a scandal of the church. He was determined he would never be open to this accusation. As patriarch of Venice, in 1955, he wrote: "I owe love, in the Lord, to my relatives, all the more so because they are poor . . . but it is important that I always live apart from them, as an example to the good clergy of

Venice who, for various reasons — some of them excusable — have too many relatives around them." When he became pope he explained to his family that he could no longer even correspond with them; if need be, they could write to his secretary. His will states: "To my beloved family, from whom indeed I have received nothing" — the last word crossed out and replaced by "no material wealth." He left them less than $20 apiece. Roncalli considered that to benefit his family was a form of pride — and a form which would come only too easily to one of his nature. It was also a betrayal of his vocation as a priest. He tackled the problem early in his adolescence, as his diary reveals; it was part of the maturing process.

Pride was directly linked to obedience. A priest is taught that pride is the greatest and most insidious sin of all, because it is never wholly subdued, and takes on an infinity of disguises. Obedience to even the unreasonable will of superiors is the most certain way to overcome it. Roncalli was, and remained to the end, a man who loved to talk; it was in his nature to gossip, to coin epigrams, to pronounce on the problems of the day, to indulge his Bergamesque sense of wit, irony and paradox. He saw his inability to remain silent as a sin of pride, all the more tempting in that, at least at home, he was surrounded by people less educated than he, who found his opinions interesting. He must, he wrote, stop himself from showing off, curb the desire "to cut a good figure, and put on the airs of a savant." "It shall be my special study to mortify myself, to quell, above all, my self-esteem, my besetting sin." "Kitchen-gossip" was a horrendous crime, because many regarded it as comparatively innocent, but in his case it was fatal. There are many passages in his diary in which he rebukes himself for voicing opinions: "I will never, never meddle in matters concerning newspapers, bishops, topics of the day, nor take up the cudgels in defense of anything which I think is being unjustly attacked and which I think fit to champion." Roncalli grew up at the seminary during a period of acute ecclesiastical controversy, much of it fascinatingly local: a canon of the cathedral had brought an action against the bishop in the Vatican courts. The young seminarian was anxious to suppress his views even on topics which concerned his cloth, and where discussion was natural, even becoming. He was much influenced, in this respect, by his spiritual director at the seminary, the Redemptorist Father Francesco Pitocci. Roncalli wrote some years later: "He used to say, and repeated even in recent times, that it is better for a young cleric to be somewhat strait-laced than incline to broadmindedness . . . he rightly considered that this youthful austerity, aided by later experience, was the best way of finding the exact middle point where truth, justice and charity meet."

In many respects this was an excellent training for Roncalli. He forced himself to be obedient and silent before his superiors. He kept his thoughts to himself, measuring and altering them against his observation of the world. The nature of the old-fashioned seminary course he underwent made it hard for students to mature, either spiritually or intellectually. The academic theology they were taught bore no apparent relation to the devotional exercises drilled into them; the liturgy in which they participated had remained virtually unchanged for three hundred years, and did not touch on life at any point. They were bidden to imitate to the letter the childlike behavior of such "perfect" saints as Saint Aloysius, Saint John Berchmans and Saint Stanislas Kostka — incredible prodigies of sanctity whose habits and prayers have dismayed or even nauseated generations of Catholic schoolboys. The wonder is that Roncalli survived this debilitating atmosphere of static, mindless religiosity with his intellectual common sense, and his spontaneous spirituality, more or less intact. But he was a strong character; he was all of a piece, even as a young man. He did as he was told. But he made up his own mind, even if he voiced his conclusions only in private writing. He rejected the exact imitation of certain saints as devotionally absurd: "From the saints I must take the substance, not the accidents, of their virtues. I am not St Aloysius, nor must I seek holiness in his particular way, but according to the requirements of my own nature, my own character."

The truth is that Roncalli was an egoist, but an egoist with self-knowledge. There was a time and a place for obedience; there would also, if God willed it, come a time for the acceptance of responsibility; there was always a time for self-examination and self-criticism. He could not reject ambition completely without destroying his character, and thus his capacity to serve. His notes reflect a recurring cycle. He speculates on doing well in exams, on becoming a famous jurist or theologian. Then he reminds himself that place is unimportant and submission to God's will is all. Then the cycle starts up again. These notes may strike us as naive, since able and ambitious men do not normally write down such thoughts, as he had been trained to do. But they also show the evolution of a mature attitude to power — power is not to be despised, but used, not to be overrated but justly considered. Roncalli knew how to use power when the time came to exercise it, and how to delegate it to others. By thinking seriously and honestly about power over a long period, he made himself virtually incorruptible when it was given to him. A passage written during a retreat in April 1903 shows him considering three elements in his mind: his imagination, which he terms "the crazy inmate"; his "reasonable, reasoning mind, my own real mind"; and "the other reasoning mind, which is my inveterate foe." He drew a useful distinction between self-sustaining egoism and egoism directed to an honorable purpose. The second must not be killed; indeed its survival inspired the radiant projection of character which made Roncalli such a successful pontiff. He lacked the capacity, or the desire, to subject his motives to subtle analysis, and reanalysis — one reason why, as a chief executive, he found decision-taking so easy, and was so little worried by afterthoughts. But he found no difficulty in making salient distinctions in reviewing his conduct. He had a strong and clear, though never brilliant, mind, made formidable by his energy and capacity for work. His problem, and he knew it, was to discipline his mind by the simplicity of faith and piety. It was his success in doing it, without any sacrifice of reason, which made him appeal so strongly to ordinary people, and yet allowed him to retain the respect of intellectuals.

In January 1901, aged nineteen, Roncalli moved from the Bergamo seminary to Rome, to complete his theology.

In the seventeenth century, a wealthy canon of Bergamo, Flaminio Cerasoli, had endowed a college in Rome for seminarians from Bergamo, which was now part of the Pontifical Seminary, though the Bergamese lived a somewhat separate existence and were notorious for their austerity and hard work. Many of Roncalli's contemporaries were well-born and connected. For a poor boy like him to complete his training in Rome was an undoubted privilege, and no doubt too the reward for industry and self-discipline. His open manners made him many friends; Roncalli never lacked powerful contacts once he began to climb the ecclesiastical ladder. He made no mistakes. He declined to read forbidden works of theology, even though they circulated at the college. In 1903, he watched the puffs of smoke which announced the election of Pius X, and was present at his coronation. Giuseppe Sarto also came from northern Italy, and from even lower social origins than Roncalli, and raised himself to become a saintly and reactionary pope. His pontificate increased the pressure on the more progressive elements within the church, and the Rome where Roncalli learned to be a priest was disturbed by bitter controversy and witch-hunting.

In this atmosphere, Roncalli prudently kept his head down, did as he was told, and concentrated on his work. He drew what spiritual nourishment he could from devotions to particular saints, always associated in his mind with historical situations and places. If he had one abiding interest throughout life, it was a fascination for the minutiae of ecclesiastical history, to which he brought the passion of a genuine antiquarian. He also took his ordination, at the statutory age of twenty-two, with great seriousness. He considered that the priesthood was the central privilege of the clerical life, and he liked to buttress it with historical associations. His behavior at the time of his ordination, in August 1904, was very characteristic of his approach. On the eve, he visited a series of shrines, and then went to Saint John Lateran, the Cathedral of Rome, to repeat his vows. Next, he climbed the Scala Santa on his knees, and ended up at Saint Paul's Outside the Walls, the supposed tomb of Saint Paul, from which he was later to announce the calling of the Ecumenical Council. He was ordained on the feast of Saint Laurence, in the church of Santa Maria in Monte Santo, on the corner where the Corso of Rome enters the Piazza del Populo. Afterwards, he wrote formal letters to his bishop and his family, and went on a further round of visits to churches and shrines, including the tomb of Saint Philip Neri in the Chiesa Nuova. The following day he went twice to Saint Peter's: first, to say mass in the crypt over the tomb of Saint Peter, where he repeated one of his favorite devotional sayings: "Lord, you know everything; you know that I love you"; later he attended a semipublic audience of Pope Pius X, who spoke kindly to him, asked him when he was going to celebrate his first mass at home, and said: "How those fine Bergamesque bells will peal out on that day!" For the next week there was a series of symbolic visits: to the summer home of the seminary, where he said mass and a sermon was preached in his honor by his spiritual director: "He was too kind in what he said of me — his affection blinded him a little"; on 13 August he said mass at the Santissima Annunziata in Florence, and on the following day at the tomb of Saint Charles Borromeo in Milan. He had already preached his first sermon, having repeated it the night before in the confessional; it was, he recorded, "a disaster." On 15 August, the Assumption, he was back home in Sotto il Monte, to say his first mass in front of his family.

These activities are worth recording at length because they illustrate the nature of the church in which Roncalli grew up, and his own attachment to those elements of its devotional life he found congenial. Roncalli was in most respects a self-assured man; but he was not self-contained, or in spiritual terms self-sufficient. He believed he needed this form of spiritual assistance. He was not ignorant of the world. Three years before he had done a year of compulsory military service in the Military Hospital at Bergamo, which he termed his Babylonian Captivity. He had been grievously shocked by the barrack-room atmosphere: "I shudder at the very thought of it," he wrote. "What blasphemies there were in that place, and what filth. . . . Oh, the world is so ugly and filthy and loathsome! In my year of military service I have learned all about it." Roncalli was never under any illusion that the life of a priest in the world was one of continuous difficulty; no aids to devotion were to be despised. It was part of his self-knowledge that he knew he needed them. He continued to scourge himself in his diary. He described his "capital" as "sin after sin — there are my title deeds." "Ah Good Lord," he wrote, "am I then, even I, destined for Hell? The poor and ignorant man in paradise, and the Turk and the savage; and I, called at the

first hour, brought up in your family, even I destined for
Hell, among the demons?" He was desperately afraid of
careerism: ". . . woe betide me if, even in the smallest
degree, I become attached to the goods of this world. As
for the dreams which my pride may depict for me, such
as honour, position, etc., I shall be very careful not to
harbour them . . . I ought to concentrate on keeping
myself humble, humble, humble . . ." If Roncalli was
strongly, perhaps over-dramatically, conscious of his
pride, this was a valuable fault for an able young man,
who had evidently made an excellent impression in Rome
and, among other things, had carried off the prize for
Hebrew studies. One way of curbing his pride was to
adopt the devotional exercises of the humble type of
Christian, something he maintained until death, and
which gave him permanent and solid links with the multitudes. Roncalli matured into a pastor who could establish relationships with all sorts and conditions; but
this sprang not merely from his nature but from his disciplined exercises — he had to work at it, as his diary
bears constant, and sometimes touching, witness.

To all outward appearances, Father Roncalli was an
able, hard-working but thoroughly conventional priest; a
very ordinary unit in the great clerical machine of Rome.
He planned to continue studies in canon law at the
Apolinaris Institute, and he might well have become a
genial, orthodox clerical lawyer, rising slowly through
the apparatus of the Curia and the Rota. Early in 1905,
however, he was invited to assist at the consecration, by
Pius X, of the new bishop of Bergamo, Count Radini-
Tedeschi. Almost immediately afterwards, Radini asked

him to come north as his secretary. Thus Roncalli entered, for the first time — though at the periphery — the world of clerical politics, and he entered it in circumstances which ensured he would lean towards the progressive faction.

TWO

The Progressive Tradition

THE STRUGGLE within the Roman Catholic church during
the last century and more has revolved in essence around
two rival propositions. Should the church attempt to affect an accommodation with the modern world which it
finds in many respects morally repugnant? Or should it
turn its back on this world, continue to preach its ancient
doctrines in all their purity, and wait for the intervention of Divine Providence to bring the world to its senses?
Should the church be an open city, or a closed fortress?
Or, to put it another way, should it radiate a spirit of
optimism or adopt a defensive posture of pessimism? The
conflict needs to be examined in some detail, for it had a
considerable bearing on Angelo Roncalli's clerical career,
and he eventually aligned himself decisively with one of
the factions.

The argument raged over many issues, but two were
preeminent. The first concerned the role of the pope as a

temporal sovereign, and in particular the relationship of the papacy with the new united Italian state. Its formation had stripped the Holy See of all its territories in Central Italy, except the enclave of the Vatican. Pius IX, who reigned from 1846–1878, and his three successors, Leo XIII (1878–1903), Pius X (1903–1914) and Benedict XV (1914–1922), refused to accept this loss of their territories and declined to acknowledge the legitimacy of the new state. An arrangement was not, in fact, reached until 1929, and until then the popes, by their own volition, remained, as they termed it, "prisoners in the Vatican." Moreover, for many decades after the formation of modern Italy, the popes not only boycotted the new state themselves but insisted that all faithful Italian Catholics do likewise by abstaining from voting in elections. This had the effect of placing the government of Italy in predominantly secularist hands, and thus deepening the gulf between the church and the state; it also inhibited the development of Christian democratic parties, not only in Italy but in France, Germany, Austria and Spain. Catholics were commanded to stand aside from the modern political process, in reproachful silence, until the world came to its senses, and acknowledged the papal claims. But, of course, the world did not come to its senses, and the long delay before the Vatican adjusted to the fact was responsible for much of the sickness in European politics both before and after the First World War: Mussolini and Hitler were the prime beneficiaries of the papal policy of exclusion.

If the papacy rejected the political arrangements of the modern world, it was even more hotly and systematically opposed to its intellectual developments, particularly those which had any bearing on its theological, moral or social teaching. Rome set its face not merely against science and scholarship emanating from secular sources, but against Catholic scholars using modern methods to explore Christian knowledge within the framework of traditional belief. Here again, Pius IX laid down the main lines of policy. In 1864 he published, as an appendix to his encyclical *Quanta Cura*, what was known as "The Syllabus of Errors," that is, a list of propositions which no good Catholic should hold or defend. The precise authority of the Syllabus was open to argument, since it was in effect nothing more than an index, giving references to all the various assertions Pius had already condemned in speeches, addresses, letters and encyclicals. But its importance was enhanced when, in 1870, the First Vatican Council formulated the doctrine of Papal Infallibility. Political circumstances prevented the council from concluding its agenda, and in particular from defining the countervailing rights of the college of bishops. Thus the council left the papacy on a lonely eminence, with all the threads of Catholic teaching firmly in its hands. The Syllabus appeared as the sole framework within which Catholics could adjust to the world, and it was uncompromising in its harshness. Sections 1–7 condemned pantheism, naturalism and absolute rationalism; 8–14 moderate rationalism; 15–18 indifferentism, latitudinarianism, socialism, communism, secret societies, Bible societies, and clerical groups connected with liberalism. In a series of sections, 19–76, the rights of the church, in their most triumphalist form, were set out, and infringements by civil society roundly condemned. The "Roman pontiff's civil princedom" was upheld, and its right to employ force defended; Catholics were forbidden to accept civil education, or to deny the assertion that the "Catholic religion was the sole religion of the state to the exclusion of all others"; in Section 79 the general freedom of speech was condemned as leading to "the corruption of manners and minds" and "the pest of indifferentism." Finally, Section 80 summed up the debate in a comprehensive manner by condemning the assertion that "the Roman pontiff can and should reconcile and harmonize himself with progress, with liberalism, and with recent civilisation."

The Syllabus was, by definition, wholly negative in its approach. And Pius IX ignored the advice of Mgr. Georges Darboy, archbishop of Paris, who wrote to him: "You have distinguished and condemned the principal errors of our epoch. Turn your eyes now to what she may hold that is honourable and good, and sustain her in her generous efforts." The effect of Pius's teaching, therefore, was to paralyze the church, and to preempt the process of adjustment by which any great institution faces the evolution of society. It tied the hands of Pius's successors on a number of practical points, an intolerable situation from which they extricated themselves by the dishonest process of ignoring it: thus, by signing the Lateran Treaty with the Italian State in 1929, Pius XI broke the injunctions in Sections 75–76, and, more recently, the injunction dealing with relations with the Eastern churches has been broken; but these undeniable breaches have never been alluded to in Vatican documents. Even more important, however, was the effect of the Syllabus in setting the tone of Roman Catholicism: any innovation, however innocent or defensible, was automatically suspect, and only the rigidly orthodox were safe.

Moreover, the cumulative effect of Pius IX's long pontificate was to give an enormous and long-lasting impetus to conservatism within the church, for promotions, particularly in the Italian church — which supplied not only the popes themselves but the great bulk of the Curia officials — were increasingly determined by the credentials of absolute orthodoxy. His successor, Leo XIII, was judged by the prevailing standards to have an element of liberalism in him. His encyclical *Rerum novarum* of 1891 has often been considered as the foundation of modern Catholic social teaching. But in fact it was only issued after great pressure from Catholic social movements in the United States, Britain, France and Germany, and it did little more than acknowledge certain assumptions that the modern world had long taken for granted. The worker had a right to a wage which would keep him and his family in decency (Leo was worried by the moral evils arising from a family sleeping in one bedroom); he could strike only in the last resort, and violence in any form was never permissible. There is nothing in Leo's teaching which indicates he had any real desire to come to terms with the world, though he was prepared, *in extremis*, to acknowledge its practices in certain cases.

His secretary of state, Cardinal Rampolla, was of a more adventurous turn of mind, and the feeling in the church that a more progressive approach was overdue made him the favorite in the conclave held after Leo's death in 1903. On the first ballot he emerged clearly head of the field with twenty-nine votes out of sixty-two, and it was evident that his lead would increase as the voting proceeded. But Rampolla had antagonized the Austrian Emperor by giving some support to Italian claims to territories in North Italy still held by Austria. After the first ballot, Cardinal Puzyna, bishop of Cracow, exercised the "Aulic Exclusiva," the veto on a papal candidate which traditionally belonged to Austria as the residual legatee of the Holy Roman Empire. The conclave did not formally acknowledge the right of veto; but the secretary to the conclave, Archbishop Merry del Val, who managed the balloting, and who was strongly opposed to Rampolla, ensured that it took effect. Rampolla's vote rose to thirty on the fourth ballot, but thereafter it fell; and the opposition to him concentrated on Cardinal Sarto, patriarch of Venice, who received twenty-four on the fourth, twenty-seven on the fifth, thirty-five on the sixth, and went well over the two-thirds majority required on the seventh.

Giuseppe Sarto, Pius X, was the son of the lowest and most despised category of civil servant, a municipal process-server and debt-collector. His background made him a rigid upholder of authority in its most brutal form, and made him profoundly skeptical of the claims of the working class to social and political rights. He was highly superstitious, believing he possessed second sight and other miraculous powers. He was a big, handsome man, with huge feet (his gigantic papal slippers can still be seen in Rome). As pope he used to lend his red socks to sufferers from foot complaints, and thus effected many cures, though oddly enough he could not cure his own uricaemia. After his death, testimony about his miracles brought him canonization. More important, for our purposes, was that the circumstances of his rise in the church greatly strengthened his conservative temperament. As bishop of Mantua he had been confronted by a city dominated by socialists and liberal Freemasons, and he had fought bitter battles with both. As patriarch of Venice, he had been prevented from taking up his duties for three years by the opposition of the Italian government. And he had become pope as the candidate of the reactionaries, and through the intervention of a foreign autocracy.

As his secretary of state, he appointed the man who had been, in effect, his electoral agent, Merry del Val. The latter was only thirty-eight, the rich son of a Spanish ambassador and an English mother; a great social figure at the European courts, a fine shot and accomplished linguist, the president of the Pontifical Academy for Noble Ecclesiastics (which supplied the Vatican diplomatic service), and a man devoted by birth and conviction to the *ancien régime*. The combination of a reactionary pope, and a conservative intellectual as his chief minister, not only crushed the very tentative liberalism of the Leonine regime, but brought about a reign of terror against progressive Catholics, which in some respects was more pervasive than anything experienced under Pius IX.

In his first encyclical, Pius stated: "We will take the greatest care to safeguard our clergy from being caught up in the snares of modern scientific thought," and he followed this by commanding that the teaching of philosophy at all seminaries should adhere strictly to the medieval methods of Aquinas. In July 1907 he published the decree *Lamentabili*, a similar document to the Syllabus of Errors, which condemned sixty-five propositions of what was termed the Modernist Heresy. Two months later his encyclical *Pascendi Gregis* widened the area of the witch-hunt by imposing an anti-Modernist oath, which all Catholic teachers, bishops and priests were obliged to take. These official efforts to extirpate heresy were accompanied, and envenomed, by the activities of a secret group in the Vatican, called the Sodalitium Pianum, and nicknamed La Sapinière. Its organizer was Mgr. Umberto Benigni, a former professor of Diplomatic Style at the Pontifical Academy, and a creature of del Val's at the Secretariat of State. Benigni was a fanatic, who believed in the existence of a "Modernist conspiracy" plotting to engulf the church for diabolical purposes. In fact the only conspiracy was the one he operated himself, for his group sought both to promote "reliable" friends and associates, and to block the promotion of "suspects." It had agents throughout the church, who communicated in code (Pius himself was "Michael," del Val was "George," and so forth), and who sought to produce evidence of heretical views, which was then referred to the Holy Office to set up prosecutions. How far del Val was privy to its operations is not clear. He broke up the group in 1913 when rumors of its activities began to circulate; but the full extent of its operations was not grasped until some of its documents fell into German hands in 1915. In the meantime, it had served to terrorize or emasculate those elements in the church who wished to deviate, even within the limits of orthodoxy, from the attitudes of Pope Pius and his secretary of state.

Now among these was the new bishop of Bergamo, Radini. He was a noble from Piacenza, a tall, thin man, with a stiff military bearing and exquisite manners. He had attended the Pontifical Academy, but had declined to go into diplomacy. Both Leo XIII and Cardinal Rampolla, whose protégé he was, had encouraged his desire to specialize in the social work of the church. This took the form of organizing, on behalf of the Vatican, the Catholic social groups, known as the Opera dei Congressi, which were the only form of public activity which Rome would permit Catholic laymen to undertake. Their object was two-fold: to bring into existence a Catholic network which could spring into political action the moment the papacy decided to allow Catholics to vote, and in the meantime to implement the policy of abstention; and, secondly, to operate charities on behalf of the Catholic working class and peasantry. For the most part they were under the control of Catholic laymen, many of whom had progressive views. Bergamo had played a leading part in this movement. Four years before Roncalli was born, the Fourth Congress of Italian Catholics had been held there, and Bergamo had taken a lead in organizing the Catholic penetration of the workers. By 1895, by which time Roncalli was studying at the seminary, there were over 200 groups, with 42,000 members, in the region. The Catholic newspapers on which he was brought up, the atmosphere in the seminary, reflected the ideals of the Opera movement.

But, paradoxically, though Bergamo took a lead in

propagating the progressive notions of the Opera, it also prided itself on being what it termed "the most Catholic diocese in Italy," the most devoted in obedience to the papacy. It had taken the lead in implementing the *non expedit* policy of Pius IX, and claimed the largest number of abstentions in the national elections; in 1890, when Roncalli was nine, eighty percent of the Bergamese abstained, and his local paper, *L'Eco*, wrote: "Our watchword is absolute submission to the pope."

On 28 July 1904, del Val struck a decisive blow against the Opera. With Pius X's approval, he sent out a letter dissolving the organization, and placing all its activities under the diocesan bishops. An exception was made for Bergamo, but its lay structure was allowed to continue only under the control of a conservative nobleman, Count Medolago-Albani, a reliable friend of the pope's. Six months later, Radini was removed from his position as national organizer of the work, and made bishop of Bergamo. He was on friendly terms with Pius, though they differed strongly on social and political issues, and at the time of his appointment they had a curious conversation. Evidently the conservatives had been trying to get Radini out of the center of events for some time. The usual method employed to neutralize a leading Curia official who cannot reasonably be accused of heresy is to "promote" him to an archbishopric. Pius told Radini: "You have been proposed for the Archbishopric of Palermo. I refused. For Ravenna: I again refused. For Bergamo: this time I agreed. Off you go. So far as it is possible to console a bishop, let me say that Bergamo is the first diocese in Italy." What he did not add, though therein

lay the sting of the appointment, was that he was sending
Radini to the one diocese in Italy where he would not
have control of the social movement, now vested in "safe"
conservative hands.

We may assume that the new bishop selected Roncalli
as secretary because he wanted someone close to him
whom he knew shared his general views, and who was
absolutely trustworthy. The two men quickly established
a close, father-and-son relationship, which was maintained until Radini's death in 1914. The bishop was a
man of enormous energy. Forbidden to devote himself to
the social work he craved, he took refuge in the rigorous
performance of his pastoral duties, carrying out repeated
and elaborate visitations of all the parishes in his diocese.
Roncalli traveled with him; he learned what it was to be
a model bishop. He also went with Radini on a series of
exhausting pilgrimages, to France, Germany, Austria and
Palestine, and helped the bishop with his ambitious plans
of modernization: electricity, running water, hot baths
and laboratories were installed at the seminary; a new
episcopal palace was built, and the cathedral restored.
The bishop and his secretary spent most of their time
together, even on holidays. Among high-minded celibate
clergy, deprived by their vocation of a truly intimate
human bond, there is room for strong feelings of affection, in no sense carnal, but of great comfort and mutual
support — this was one of them. Roncalli nursed the
bishop through his last illness. Told he was dying of
cancer, Radini, who was only in his fifties, lost heart, and
said he could not face the judgment of God. Roncalli
comforted him, and administered the last rites: as he

listened to the prayers, the bishop composed himself, and said (his last words): *"Ecco qua, il mio uomo coraggioso e forte"* — "here he is, my courageous and strong fellow."

It was natural for Roncalli to write his master's biography. It is a work of piety, though Roncalli does not conceal the bishop's faults: rashness, obstinacy, an occasional outburst against the enemies of the church (Roncalli, as pope, used to say to himself: "The church has no enemies"). But he does not conceal his affection. "While writing the book," he says, "more than once I felt my hand trembling under the pressure of overpowering emotions, so great was the love I felt for my bishop because of the transcendent purity of his spirit and the openness of his heart." Nor does Roncalli try to hide the fact that Radini was, to some extent, the victim of the church he served. While he was recognized as an outstanding diocesan, his actions were carefully watched by his enemies in Rome, who had their informants in Bergamo. He got into trouble in 1909 by making a donation to a local strike fund, and was only exonerated by a letter from the pope, written — Roncalli tells us — in Pius's own hand. During the elections of 1913, the local policy adopted by Radini, which had been decided on after long and anxious preparation, and with the pope's initial approval, was reversed under pressure from the Curia, and Radini was forced into the humiliating position of having to repudiate it publicly. Even so, his last year was spent in an atmosphere of papal displeasure, and Roncalli hints that this was one of the causes of his early death: "A sharp thorn was driven into the heart of Mgr Radini. It drew blood, and although the bleeding was silent and concealed, it was none the less real and painful."

Roncalli wrote this passage in the knowledge that, had Radini lived, his career would certainly have taken a very different turn. Pius X had died only a few days before, and had remarked, on his deathbed, that he would "soon summon Mgr Radini to follow him." This sinister prophecy was taken as another example of Pius's "Second sight"; perhaps it was uttered with an ironic overtone, for Pius must have known that his own death opened the way to Radini's rehabilitation and promotion. In 1907, two years after he had relegated Radini to the bishopric of Bergamo, he had likewise "promoted" to the archbishopric of Bologna Radini's friend and colleague, Giacomo Della Chiesa, another protégé of the liberal Cardinal Rampolla. Della Chiesa was regarded as eminently *papabile*; for this reason, Merry del Val had blocked his elevation to the cardinalate — to which, as head of the Bologna province, he would by custom be entitled automatically — and he had only got his Red Hat in 1914 through the personal intervention of the pope. Thus Pius belatedly opened Della Chiesa's road to the papacy, and he was in due course elected, as Benedict XV. Almost his first act, as a faithful pupil of Rampolla, was to put an end to the witch-hunt against the Modernists, in his encyclical *Ad Beatissimi*. If Radini had lived, the new pope would certainly have made him a cardinal and brought him back to Rome, perhaps as secretary of state; and Roncalli would have followed in his wake, on the main road to promotion. As it was, the bishop's secretary, though a member of the progressive camp, was too little known to be singled out for favor; his master dead, he was virtually forgotten.

But his experience as Radini's lieutenant had already inured him to the vicissitudes of clerical warfare. He learned a lot from the bishop. Except during the final phase of his life, Radini took his reverses well; he was, wrote Roncalli, *vir amabilis ad societatem*, and an optimist: "There was no room in him for weariness or melancholy." He advised Roncalli to steer clear of clerical politics, and followed his own precept: "His conviction was that, today as yesterday, a bishop is the better fitted to serve religion or society if he keeps to his pastoral function, that is to say if he remains aloof from any political prejudice or intrigue . . ." Roncalli's diary during his years as the bishop's secretary continues to express his abhorrence of clerical careerism. "I must proceed," he wrote, "as my confessor tells me, with my head in the sack of Divine Providence." There were other, more compelling reasons for remaining unobtrusive. These were the worst years of the anti-Modernist terror. In addition to his duties at the palace, Roncalli lectured three times a week on ecclesiastical history at the Bergamo seminary, and the teaching staff of seminaries were the particular objects of the witch-hunt. In Autumn 1910 there is an oblique reference in the diary to the disgrace and expulsion of one of his colleagues, Don Giuseppe Moioli, on charges of modernism; and he was not the only victim at Bergamo. Roncalli's comments show that he took a safe line. What else could he do? He doubtless feared he might be asked to produce his diary for inspection, and if his remarks were not ultracautious they could be used in evidence against him. During the worst period, the bishop and Roncalli often repeated to each other the words spoken by Saint Alphonsus Liguri when the Jesuits were suppressed by the Vatican: "The Pope's will; God's will." But Roncalli also quoted with approval the bishop's saying: "There is a prudence which is boldness, and a wisdom which consists in breaking through all the obstacles which impede a straight road." On at least one occasion Roncalli took a stand. On 29 September 1911 he published in the diocesan magazine, *La Vita Diocesana*, an article criticizing a course of lectures given at the seminary by an extremist anti-Modernist. He had chosen his ground well, for the lectures had been marked by violent language and abusive attacks on individuals, including Leo XIII. Roncalli deplored these, and added: "If the truth and the whole truth had to be told, I do not see why it had to be accompanied by the thunders and lightnings of Sinai rather than the calm and serenity of Jesus on the lake and on the mount." This article was doubtless passed to the Holy Office. Shortly after Roncalli became pope, in 1958, he visited the office and asked to see his personal file. It was marked: "Suspected of Modernism."

Too prudent to involve himself in ecclesiastical controversy, Roncalli devoted his spare time, and his intellectual energies, to history. It was, in any case, more to his taste. In 1907 he gave a paper, which he later published, on Caesar Baronius, the seventeenth century cardinal, church historian and friend of Saint Philip Neri. This led him to explore the papers of Saint Charles Borromeo, Baronius's contemporary, and in particular the records of his Apostolic Visitation to Bergamo in 1575. The papers were housed in the Ambrosian Library in Milan, which Roncalli often visited, and where he struck up an acquaintance with the librarian, Achille Ratti, later Pope Pius XI. Roncalli did most of the basic work of transcription during the years before the war, and eventually published the results in five volumes, the first appearing in 1936, the last after he became pope. The work is of no great interest, and testifies chiefly to Roncalli's fascination with the minute details of the ecclesiastical past. At the time it served as a safe answer to the fanaticism of the anti-Modernists; it was respectable and worthy work, a case of "honourable survival." In the long run, Roncalli's grasp of church history played a major part in shaping his ideas as pope. "History is the teacher of life," he told the council in 1962. He saw the history of the church as a story of continual ferment, innovation and change. Only those who were ignorant of history, he argued, saw the church as a static institution, resisting change in all its forms. A historian was not fearful: he had seen it all before. And Roncalli rightly saw fear as the main dynamic behind the anti-Modernist hunt, as it had been behind all violent persecutions. He might have said, as Roosevelt was later to say: "We have nothing to fear but fear itself." The church was being paralyzed by fear; but those who studied its long history knew that fear could safely be dismissed, and trust in Divine Providence put in its place.

In the years after the bishop's death in 1914, Roncalli experienced for the first time the anguish of the "forgotten man." Benedict XV was a liberal, but the coming of war ruled out any consistent attempt to promote the interests of the progressive party in the church, or reform its structure. And the pope was a sick man, a cripple, drained of energy by constant pain. Able men like Roncalli went unnoticed. In 1915 Italy entered the war, and he was called up to serve in the Army Hospital Service, as a sergeant. He was now thirty-four, growing stout and bald; he grew a formidable black mustache — "What a mistake!" He continued to lecture at the seminary, teaching dogmatic theology and apologetics, eventually becoming its spiritual director. At the end of the war he established a hostel for lay-students at Bergamo University, a project into which he threw much energy but which soon ran into criticism for its comparatively lax discipline. He was conscious that the best years of his life were passing by, with nothing of any importance accomplished. On retreat, aged thirty-seven, he consoled himself by denouncing clerical careermanship: "Experience teaches us to beware of responsibilities. They are solemn enough in themselves if assumed under obedience, but terrifying for whoever has sought them for himself, pushing himself forward without being called upon . . . Vanity of vanities." All the same, he knew that his abilities, and his immense capacity for work, were being squandered.

In the end, it was his historical work which brought him forward again. His life of Bishop Radini was published in 1920, and he sent a complimentary copy to Radini's old friend, Pope Benedict. At the end of the year, Roncalli was suddenly summoned to Rome by Cardinal Van Rossum, head of the Vatican ministry, or Congregation, which controlled the church's missionary activities. Fund-raising for the missions had hitherto been centered at Lyons, in France. The decision had now been taken to transfer the work to Rome, and Roncalli was asked to coordinate the activities in Italy. He was selected by the pope himself, who had evidently been reminded of Roncalli's existence by reading his book. On 7 May 1921 he was appointed a papal prelate, or monsignor, and immediately afterwards elected an honorary canon of Bergamo Cathedral. It was recognition of a sort. His work was intellectually undemanding, but it took him all over Italy, and through much of western and central Europe. He became a well-known figure in Rome, and met a wide range of foreign ecclesiastical personalities. Roncalli made friends easily, and, like Dr. Johnson, he thought that "friendship should be kept in constant repair." He was now a man marked for promotion.

But less than a year later, in January 1922, Benedict died of bronchitis. At the conclave which followed, the worst was avoided. The reactionary group, led by del Val and La Fontaine, patriarch of Venice, was blocked by Cardinal Gasparri, Benedict's secretary of state, and his supporters. They swung their votes behind a compromise candidate, Cardinal Ratti, who was elected pope after a long and bitter battle, on the fourteenth ballot. Ratti was an undistinguished offspring of the Lombard middle class, a trained librarian and archivist, a bit of a mountaineer in his spare time. He was well disposed to scholars, provided their work was uncontroversial, and he restored the Papal Academy of Science. But in politics and theology he was gullible and conservative. He had no time at all for the Christian Democrat movement, in Italy or elsewhere. In France he tended to back the reactionary Catholics gathered round Action Française, even though its leader, Charles Maurras, was an avowed agnostic, who saw the church simply as a bastion against the Left. Pius had no sympathy for the Christian Progressives of Germany, where politics was polarizing between the Socialists and the Communists on the one hand, and the *revanchistes* who eventually handed power to Hitler. In Italy, Don Sturzo, with the encouragement of Benedict XV, had established the Partito Populare as a mass-party of Christian workers. Pius XI gave it no countenance, and after Mussolini marched on Rome in October 1922, the pope decided to back him with the object of settling the "Roman Question" once and for all. This was accomplished with the signature of the Lateran Treaty in 1929; Pius proclaimed he had "given Italy back to God"; Mussolini called him "a good Italian." In the meantime, Mussolini had established his fascist dictatorship, with Pius's acquiescence. Sturzo was forced into exile in 1924, and his successor Alcide de Gasperi — who was to emerge, after the Second World War, as a remarkable Christian Democrat Prime Minister — spent four years in jail. In his old age, Pius XI was to come to hate the dictators, especially Hitler. But for much of his long pontificate (1922–1939) his attitude towards them was ambivalent, if not cordial.

Hence, in Pius XI's Rome, there was not much future for a man of Roncalli's views and temperament. Though his position as President for Italy of the Central Council for Papal Missions (his formal title) gave him little direct power at the Curia, it was not a post the conservatives cared to see occupied by an able and energetic man who was not of their persuasion. It may be that he was made the victim of a characteristic Vatican maneuver. In 1924 he was appointed a part-time professor of Patrology at the ultra-conservative Lateran College. He was, by now, well versed in the writings of the early doctors of the church, and competent for the task, which in any case he could not refuse without awkwardness. Nevertheless, it was an exposed position. After only one term he was removed. As usual, no reason was given; indeed, the Holy Office rarely gave its reasons to a cleric formally disciplined, other than stating the broad charges. In this case there was no charge. But a friend of Roncalli's, Dom Lambert Beauduin, later stated that Roncalli was alleged to have fallen into Modernism during his lectures, and this is very likely the explanation. At all events, it was a black mark against him, and prepared the way for his removal from Rome. The next year, 1925, he was appointed, by a personal decision of the pope, Apostolic Visitor to Bulgaria. For reasons of protocol, the post carried with it a formal promotion: Roncalli was made an archbishop, *in partibus infidelium*, that is to a provincial see, Areopolis in Palestine, where the church had ceased to function. In all other respects it was a blow. Roncalli had never been trained as a diplomat. He spoke none of the languages he would need, not even (at this date) French. Since Bulgaria had no relations with the Holy See, he was to have no official status. He knew nothing of Bulgaria or its problems. His exact role was left unclear, his instructions were vague, and no indications were given to him whether his mission was to be temporary or permanent. In Vatican terms, it was a simple case of exile.

Roncalli took from Baronius his episcopal motto: "Obedientia et Pax." It was apt in more than one respect. Roncalli was devoted to Dante, and in particular to that fine passage where the poet signifies that the only true serenity to be found on earth is submission to God's will. He had long ago grasped that no Catholic clergyman could find happiness, or even peace of mind, unless he accustomed himself to absolute obedience to his superiors, so that submission, without *arrière-pensées*, became instinctive. In his diary, which he had resumed in 1924 after a five-year interval, the words "peace" and "serenity" recur with increasing frequency, as his object in life. Above all, he stresses his need for "calmness." His earlier struggles against "putting on airs" fall into the background. He never exactly learned to hold his tongue, but he had certainly crushed vanity. The need for calmness reflects, rather, his own inner agitation of spirit, the desire to shut off his thoughts as well as his mouth. If, in the life of a great ecclesiastic, the inward quest for perfection is rightly considered to be more central than his external actions, then Roncalli's battle for composure is the most interesting and illuminating aspect of his personality. It was to be a dominant theme of the next twenty years in his career, a long-drawn "dark night of the soul."

THREE

Ecumenical Apprentice

ARCHBISHOP RONCALLI arrived in Sofia, the capital of the Bulgarian Kingdom, in April 1925, with no clear idea of what he was supposed to do. The assumption was that he would investigate the state of the Catholics there, make a report and recommendations, and then return to Rome for further duties. Bulgaria had put out feelers to Rome for a concordat in 1923; the Vatican had sent out a young French diplomati, Mgr. Eugène Tisserant, the following year, and he had recommended a more perma-nent mission: that was why Roncalli was in Sofia, in theory. But as he had not been appointed on a permanent basis, and had no official relations with the Bulgarian government, his role seemed merely to duplicate Tis-serant's. The king, Boris, had been brought up as an Orthodox Christian by his father King Ferdinand, "the Balkan Fox," to appease the Russians: this had led to a notorious audience with Leo XIII, who had dismissed him from the room with the single word: "Leave!" "He chased me out like a dog," Ferdinand complained. When war came Ferdinand sided with the Germans, and lost his throne in consequence. Roncalli found Sofia in some confusion. A week before, a bomb had been exploded in the Orthodox cathedral, blowing to pieces Boris's strong-man prime minister, Simon Gheorgiev, and nearly killing the king himself. Troops and police were on the streets: a Ruritania without the charm. Roncalli had an initial audience with Boris which lasted over three hours, and he found the king "sympathetic and cultured"; but he was not empowered to negotiate.

Roncalli's residence, 3 Linlina Street, was small and unfinished. He had virtually no staff, not even a proper secretary. There was no local bishop, no seminary. In the circumstances, he did the sensible thing, which was also what came naturally to him: he went on an exhaustive tour of the Catholic communities. They were scattered and impoverished. Over eighty-five percent of the population was Orthodox. There were 200,000 Muslims and only 50,000 Catholics, less than one percent. Moreover, they were of two, mutually hostile, kinds. The Uniates, that is, those in communion with Rome but using the Eastern rites, numbered 5,000; the rest were Latins. Some were Thracians, some Macedonians, many refugees, or what would later be termed "displaced persons." Most of the peasants were Slav nationalists, who wanted the liturgy said in old Slavonic. But the Catholic hospitals and schools had been founded by Western missionaries, mainly French, in the nineteenth century, and were still largely staffed by foreigners from various orders. The infrastructure of the church, such as it was, thus had a flavor of colonialism about it: Roncalli discovered that in most of the churches the mass was said in Latin, and the prayers and rosary in French.

From an organizational point of view, in short, Bulgaria was a mess, as Roncalli quickly discovered. He traveled all over the country, visiting the scattered villages of Latins and Uniates, using horses, horse-carriages, occasionally a car, once a cart drawn by oxen. He was dismayed by the problems, touched by the enthusiasm with which the peasants greeted him: they reminded him of home. A local newspaper, which interviewed him, reported: "The face of Mgr Roncalli lights up with real joy when he is speaking of our country and its simple, gentle peasants." It also listed the books in his room: the early Fathers, Dante, Petrarch, Manzoni, author of Roncalli's favorite novel, *I Promessi Sposi*. The "churches" he toured were often hovels, or complete ruins, the people desperately poor and ill-instructed. He was advised by the police not to wear his pectoral cross and ring, for fear they might attract brigands. He began to learn Bulgarian and French, and ordered that the communal prayers be said in the native tongue. But his efforts to reform the structure met with little success. He won the consent of Rome to consecrate a Uniate bishop, a local man, Stephan Kurteff. But his advice that Bulgarians be appointed to responsible positions among the Latin Christians — to remove the colonialist taint — was ignored by Rome. Indeed, this was impossible without a seminary, and his plan to establish one was vetoed. He received no new instructions, despite his requests, and the questions he put in his reports to Rome went unanswered.

Roncalli's diary, and his occasional letters to close friends, reflected his desolation of spirit. "My ministry has brought me many trials. But, and this is strange, they are not caused by the Bulgarians for whom I work but by the central organisation of ecclesiastical administration . . . this . . . hurts me deeply. . . . 'Set a guard over my mouth, O Lord.'" The expectation that he would soon be relieved of his duties and put to more responsible work was painfully disappointed as the years dragged on. He was lonely, without intellectual companionship, and with no one to whom he could confide his troubles. In 1930, after five years in Sofia, he complained of "the enforced restriction of my life as a complete hermit, in opposition to my longing for work directly ministering to souls." Later, in 1950, he was to recall: "In Bulgaria, the difficulties of my circumstances, even more than the difficulties caused by men, and the monotony of that life which was one long sequence of daily pricks and scratches, cost me much in mortification and silence."

Curiously enough, his mission was saved by its most notable, and disastrous, incident. In 1929, Mussolini and Cardinal Gasparri, the secretary of state, in an atmosphere of some frivolity, arranged to marry Giovanna, daughter of King Victor Emmanuel III of Italy, to King Boris. The clear understanding, as Roncalli was assured by the king on his word of honor, was that the marriage was to be solemnized solely by Catholic rites, and that the offspring would be brought up as Catholics. It took place at Assisi in October, but immediately the couple returned

to Sofia they were married again according to Orthodox
rites. Pius XI was furious, and made his indignation
public; at one point it seemed likely that Roncalli would
be asked to leave. The episode, however, gave him his
first opportunity to exercise his considerable diplomatic
powers. At the Secretariat of State he was regarded, then
and later, as a laughable amateur. In fact, he was exceptionally agile at establishing close personal relationships
without conceding issues of principle — the essence of
diplomatic method. He smoothed things down both in
Rome and Sofia — it was the only sensible course — and
as a result he got official Bulgarian recognition as a papal
delegate, and in the process a new house, which he
quickly decorated in the Bergamesque fashion. The *rapport* with Boris survived a further crisis in 1933, when
he insisted that the infant daughter of the marriage be
baptized as an Orthodox Christian. This was a further
breach of trust; indeed, Roncalli stated flatly: "The King
deceived me," and he made a formal protest. He added:
"Apart from the affair of the baptism, he is a good man.
But what a mystery the human heart is!" So it is; but
Roncalli was not one to allow differences of temperament, ideology or even moral principles to discourage
him in seeking friendship and concord, if at all possible.
As a diplomat, he had the heroic persistence of a good
man, always looking for points of agreement. They liked
him in Bulgaria, where he was known as "Monsignore
Vogliamoci Bene" — a reference to his customary form
of greeting: "Let us both wish ourselves well."

All the same, impotent exile did not grow easier with
the years. In 1933 he wrote: "The prolongation of my

life as representative of the Pope in this country often brings to me severe personal suffering which I force myself to hide." He traveled a good deal: to Greece, Turkey, Rumania, Poland, Czechoslovakia, and to Berlin, where he stayed with the nuncio, Eugenio Pacelli, later Pius XII. But always he had to return to his backward seat of exile. In letters to friends he joked: "Notwithstanding appearances to the contrary, I am like a little beast of burden, always harnessed to his little cart. I don't carry much weight, but I'm always at work." His diary tells a more somber tale, of "acute and intimate suffering," of a man "hidden from the world, perhaps forgotten by your superiors . . . little appreciated." He was mortified when, in 1933, a rumor was circulated in Rome that he was to receive a modest promotion to Bucharest; it was leaked to the press — not by him — and promptly repudiated by the secretariat, which appointed another, younger man. Roncalli again exhorted himself to display "calmness, serenity."

At the end of 1934, by which time he was fifty-four, he received promotion of a sort. His friends appear to have considered — he made no comment himself — that he was overdue for advancement up a regular step on the ladder: a fat Italian bishopric or archbishopric, or one of the important nunciatures. Instead, he was moved sideways, to Istanbul, where he was charged with the affairs of Catholics in Turkey and Greece. This was, by comparison, more congenial work. It involved residence in the great cosmopolitan city of Istanbul where he was, in effect, bishop of 10,000 Catholics of many races, his first real pastoral assignment. He had his own cathedral and a much more sophisticated organization than in Bulgaria. The Istanbul Catholics of the Latin rite had a tradition stretching back for centuries and a long history of persecution and survival. But he was also papal ambassador to the Latins of the Smyrna archdiocese, to the Armenian and Greek Catholic communities of Asia Minor and the Black Sea, and the Catholics of the Chaldean rite, controlled from their bishopric in Baghdad, to which he was also delegate. He had to deal with four different types of Christians in communion with Rome, and also with the Greek and Turkish governments, the first Orthodox and passionately anti-Italian (as· the Greeks had been since the Fourth Crusade, at the beginning of the thirteenth century), the second secularist to the point of fanaticism, and anti-Western with the first flavor of modern postcolonial touchiness. It was a complicated and difficult assignment. He grasped the point of it at once, writing to a friend, early in 1935: "Each of us has his cross to bear, and each takes its particular form. Mine is fashioned entirely in the style of this century." Roncalli was later to speak of the three concentric circles of humanity: those in communion with Rome, an outer circle of schismatics and non-Catholic Christians, and a far circle of non-Christians and agnostics. At Istanbul he had a glimpse of ecumenism in its widest sense, an excellent training for a universalist pope, for he had to deal, at varying levels of formality, with Catholics, non-Christians, both Muslim and secular, and schismatic Christians of varying degrees of hostility, as well as two governments — one, in Greece, opposed to Christianity in Rome for historical reasons, the other, in Turkey, opposed to Christianity, indeed religion, as such. And the work was both pastoral and diplomatic: when he met failures in one, he could take refuge in the other.

Roncalli was never as unhappy in Istanbul as he had been in Sofia. It was partly that he was growing older, less hypersensitive to misfortune, more resigned to unambitious routine. His work, too, was more varied, in that it involved coping with an entirely new range of difficulties, particularly in Greece. Initially, at least, the Greek government, influenced in this respect by the Orthodox hierarchy as well as growing anti-Italian feeling, was almost entirely hostile to his activities. "My mission to Greece," he wrote, "Oh, what a burden!" The Apostolic Delegation was not officially recognized when he paid his first visit to Athens in May 1935 and he had difficulty in getting a visa: it was issued to him as a tourist for eight days only. Roncalli made no *démarche*, or even an informal complaint. Indeed, in all the record of his diplomatic career, there is no instance of his lodging a protest about his status or dignity, or employing any of the customary artillery of diplomatic anger. (The only exception is the formal note of protest he delivered to the Bulgarians after the christening of Boris's daughter, and this was on the direct orders of the Holy See.) Roncalli's method was to play down or ignore difficulties, and try to circumvent them by friendly personal contacts. Although his diary registers his occasional moments of depression, in public he invariably took the optimistic view that things would certainly improve, given time and patience. In fact he soon got on terms with King George II of Greece and the senior officials at the foreign ministry, who issued him a diplomatic passport and treated him as *persona grata*. The publication of the new Greek civil code struck a heavy blow at the Catholic communities, which were small and scattered mainly in the islands, for it provided that, in cases of mixed marriage, the only officiating priest was to be Orthodox. Roncalli was unable to get the ruling changed, which had the predictable effect of reducing the number of Catholics over a period. Thanks, again, to obstruction in Rome, he failed to get a new seminary built. But he took comfort in another of his favorite mottoes: *omnia videre, multa dissimulare, pauca corrigere* — see everything, ignore a good deal, improve things where possible. If all else failed, he concentrated on friendly gestures, to show good will. He visited a number of famous Orthodox monasteries and churches, the first Latin prelate to do so for many years; of course he went unofficially, but his pilgrimages aroused much favorable comment in Orthodox circles; to suspicious Rome they could be represented as made from mere antiquarian interest. He used to describe his attempts to establish better relations by a multitude of such little gestures as "ant's work, bee's work."

In Turkey the Ataturk regime was strongly xenophobic and anticlerical, and committed to a systematic policy of secularization. The government saw itself as the representative of an exploited and humiliated people, determined to throw off the yoke both of foreign colonialism and religious obscurantism. It viewed the mainly French-speaking expatriate Catholic community in Istanbul with suspicion, and the papal delegate as a potential enemy. Of course its main religious animus was directed against the Muslim Imamate, but Christian clergy of all denominations were also the object of penal laws. Among other things, it forbade all clergy to wear religious dress in public. Roncalli was, throughout his life, a stickler for the sartorial proprieties; as A. J. Balfour said of Mr. Gladstone, he was "a conservative in all but essentials." He thought the clergy should dress according to their ecclesiastical station, in obedience to canon law, and he found the enforced use of civil clothes personally irksome. But he obeyed the new law in full, and without registering any complaint, though this sometimes involved changing his clothes several times a day. The French ambassador was less prudent. He delivered a formal complaint, on behalf of the religious orders, against the sumptuary regulations, and was grimly told: "Capitulations have been out of fashion for some time here: we are the masters of Turkey now." If the French cared to send gunboats, they would be assured of a warm reception. Roncalli was more worried by the law banning religious publications, and by state interference in the Catholic schools. Many of the latter had to be closed down, and some religious orders withdrew from Turkey altogether.

Roncalli's official relations with the Turkish government were virtually nonexistent to begin with, and he was advised not to call on the foreign ministry. But he struck up friendships with various members of the Turkish government and civil service, and he found the Turks, at any rate in private, warm and responsive provided their new-found dignity was respected. Unlike most of the international community in Istanbul, he made no fuss about the transfer of the capital to Ankara. He told the under-secretary at the foreign ministry: "I always prefer to dwell on the things which make for unity, rather than on those which tend to separate." He produced two more of his mottoes: *Gutta cavat lapidem* — drops wear away a stone — and *Dabo frontem meam persecutientibus* — turn the other cheek. Once again he concentrated on little gestures. He learned a bit of Turkish, and used it for some of his official documents. He had part of the Gospel and some prayers read in Turkish.

Roncalli enjoyed his pastoral work; it was the first time he had functioned as a bishop. His predecessor, Archbishop Margotti, had been tactless and interfering and had created tension between the delegation and the local Latins. Roncalli's tact and good spirits soon restored peace. He also engaged in ecumenical work which, by the standards of prewar Catholicism, was adventurous and almost unprecedented. In 1939, after careful preparation, he contrived to pay a call on the headquarters of the Orthodox hierarchy, in the Phanar, or lighthouse district of Istanbul. The same year, on the death of Pius XI, he organized a joint service of commemoration in his cathedral, at which Orthodox, Armenian and Jewish clergy were present. The occasion was multilingual as well as multireligious, with blessings being given by various prelates in Greek, Turkish and Bulgarian as well as Latin.

Relations with the Curia continued to be difficult, and there can be little doubt that he felt himself to be the victim of a systematic, though never sensational, persecution. On retreat in 1936 he wrote: "I wish to continue always to render good for evil, and in all things to endeavor to prefer the Gospel truth to the wiles of human politics." By "human politics" he meant Vatican intrigues. In one respect, however, he felt the Holy See had treated him handsomely. He had spent his accumulated savings on major improvements in the official residence, redecorating it in his beloved Bergamesque style. His superiors insisted on refunding him the money. With the cash, and through the good offices of Monsignor (later Cardinal) Agagianian, he secured a complete set, some 350 volumes, of Migne's *Patrologia Latina* and *Patrologia Graeca,* and presented this munificent gift to the Bergamo seminary. But this was an isolated example of Vatican generosity. The diplomatic hierarchy, as a rule, treated him as a forgotten man. Once, he was driven to write a twenty-page letter of complaint, which was shown to the pope, evoking the comment: *"Ecce ira agni"* — behold the wrath of the lamb. More often, though, "calmness, serenity" prevailed over justified anger. By 1940 Roncalli was in his sixtieth year, and reflected in his diary that he was entering old age. The prospect did not daunt him; indeed, he thought that, in some ways, it was an improvement. "I feel something more mature and authoritative in me in relation to all that interests and surrounds me. I think I notice greater detachment from all that concerns my own future, a more marked indifference 'to all created things,' persons, places and undertakings to which I was once strongly attached, a more evident inclination to understand and sympathise, and a greater tranquillity and clarity in impressions and judgments." The next year he sent a photo of himself to a friend, writing on the back: "Here is Mgr Roncalli, aged 60. This is the best age: sound health, a more mature judgment, a disposition to see

things more clearly, to judge with gentleness and optimism." He had now been *en poste* for over fifteen years,
with no recognition whatever for his work; but "I am
not yet, thanks be to God, obsessed with the idea of ob-
taining a cardinal's hat."

The election of Cardinal Pacelli as Pope Pius XII in
1939 brought no change in Roncalli's standing with the
Curia. Pacelli, as secretary of state during Pius XI's last
years, had held most of the reins of papal government in
his hands, and his succession was almost automatic. More
intellectual than his predecessor, he was equally conservative, and there was no room for progressives at his court.
In any case, Vatican politics were soon dominated by the
war. Pius XII was a passionate Germanophile, and he
viewed the Western allies with coldness if not actual hostility, especially after Italy entered the war on the side
of the Nazis, and Hitler invaded the Soviet Union. Pius
saw Soviet communism as an infinitely greater threat
than naziism to Christian civilization, and both his public
attitudes and his private diplomacy were conditioned by
this fundamental belief. Roncalli, then and later, was
extremely loath to make any comments on Pius XII's
wartime policies. At best, they were morally ambiguous,
but Roncalli, following his usual practice, was inclined to
give Pius the benefit of the doubt and assume that he
acted for the best, according to his lights. Certainly, as
pope, Roncalli deplored the personal attacks on his predecessor's good name; but the fact that he declined to
publish the relevant Vatican documents, some of which
appeared after his death, suggests that, in his view, they
did not show Pius in a favorable light.

At the time, the war, while making Roncalli's pastoral work more difficult, greatly enhanced his diplomatic importance. His movements were circumscribed, but Istanbul was an arena where both sides of the conflict met in uneasy neutrality and where there were constant opportunities for the mediatory work for which Roncalli was excellently qualified, by his position and still more by his temperament. Very little is known about his wartime career, and it is most improbable that he was privy to Pius's diplomacy, except insofar as it affected the Istanbul delegation directly. But it is fair to say that the war years, for the first time, enabled Roncalli to make a real impression on the Curia, and thus opened his way to promotion. Without the war, it is very improbable that Roncalli would have become pope: thus Providence, as he might have said, works in mysterious ways.

His own attitude was to be friends to all and enemies to none. He had no sympathy for the Mussolini regime — on the contrary — and regarded Italy's entry into the war as a national disaster. But his love for his country was strong, and increased as the disasters fell upon it, and it was sometimes an effort to conceal his feelings at the sufferings of the Italian people. He wrote: "It is one thing to love Italy, as I most fervently do, and quite another to display this affection in public." He added, in a phrase which was to epitomize his own diplomacy as pope: "The Holy Church, which I represent, is the mother of nations, all nations." The record of his meditations made during a retreat, in November 1940, shows that he did not believe it was the nature of God to "take sides" in war; He did not intervene: "even His assistance to His church, al-

though it preserves her from final defeat, does not guarantee her immunity from trials and persecutions."

Roncalli was dismayed by the Italian invasion of Greece,
and noted that the Greeks, who had called their Latin
enemies "Franks" since the days of the Fourth Crusade,
now referred to them as "Italians." After the Nazis came
to the rescue of the Italians, and completed the conquest,
they handed over much of the administration of the
country to the Italian military authorities, and this in-
tensified the hatred and contempt with which Italians
were regarded, and from which, naturally, Roncalli suffered. He was obliged, on his visits to Greece, both to
minister to the occupying forces and to carry on his normal work with the Greek Catholics. The fact that he managed to remain on good terms with both testifies to his
tact and warm-heartedness. Roncalli was a hard man to
dislike at all; impossible to dislike for long. In the end,
he was able to render the Greeks an important service,
by negotiating with the Allies a lifting of the blockade,
which allowed grain ships to reach the Piraeus during the
famine of winter 1941. This was perhaps his most significant wartime achievement. But there were many others.
Istanbul was an important staging-post in various chan-
nels through which Jews were smuggled to safety from
Occupied Europe; it was also a place where deals to ex-
change Jews for raw materials were arranged. Roncalli
played a major, though very discreet, part in these arrangements. Unlike Pius XII, he had immense sympathy
for the Jewish people, which was later to find public expression in the "Declaration of the Jews" which he and
Cardinal Bea drew up for the Vatican Council. At the

time, his views found more concrete expression in saving Jewish lives. He kept on good terms with the German ambassador, Franz von Papen, who was ambivalent towards the Nazi cause and anxious to secure hostages to fortune if, as he believed, it would be lost. Roncalli's contacts with Papen ensured that the German embassy made little effort to interfere in the mercy-traffic in Jews. Even more notable, in a sense, was the delegate's efforts to hold the ring among the French, who formed the largest and richest element in the cosmopolitan community of Latins in Istanbul, and were bitterly divided into Gaullist and Pétainiste factions. Again, he contrived to remain on terms with both, negotiated between them, and prevented open warfare.

It was undoubtedly this last service which determined the form that Roncalli's promotion took. If his wartime efforts had been noted with approval in Rome, he was himself unaware of any change of feeling towards him. He was sixty-three in 1944, when the tide turned decisively in favor of the Allies. In terms of his career he was virtually at the end of the road, or so it seemed; the best he could hope for was semiretirement to a minor Italian see. On 6 December he received a coded telegram from the Vatican. His cipher clerk was off duty and the archbishop decoded it himself. It instructed him to proceed without delay to Paris, to take up the post of nuncio to the new French government. Roncalli was so astonished that he assumed he had made a mistake in the decoding; the return of his clerk confirmed this was not so. Roncalli was not the only one to be taken aback; Archbishop Tardini, acting secretary of state, later told him: "It came as a surprise to us, too." It was a personal decision of the pope, but from Pius's point of view it made perfectly good sense. In a Europe which was changing beyond recognition, he was reaping the whirlwind which he and his predecessors had sown, before and during the war. In his great need, he was turning to a man whom he, and his faction in the church, had kept out in the cold for twenty years. The appointment reflected neither approval nor regard: just necessity. Roncalli had no time to reflect on this abrupt change of fortune. He made a hurried series of farewells to the various groups in his apostolate, and then took off in a ramshackle aircraft the French had placed at his disposal. He reached Paris just in time to offer the government New Year greetings on behalf of the diplomatic corps, of which he was, *ex officio*, the dean. He was now on the world stage.

FOUR

❦

Quai d'Orsay

OVER THE CENTURIES, France has caused the Holy See more anxiety than any other part of Christendom, and, also, provided more stimulus to the growth of Christian ideas and ecclesiology. France was, and is, "the eldest daughter of the Church," its king "His Most Christian Majesty"; as Roncalli liked to put it, quoting an old saying of Cardinal Pie, "Italy is St Peter, France is St Paul." France had produced the Cluniac revival of Monasticism, the Cistercian movement, and had first preached the Crusades; France had contributed, among scores of other leading saints, Saint Bernard, Saint Vincent de Paul, Saint John Vianney, Saint Bernadette, Saint Thérèse of Lisieux; France had created the modern missionary evangelism. France had also, in the fourteenth century, been responsible for the "Babylonian Captivity" of the papacy in Avignon. In the late sixteenth century France had nearly turned Protestant; in the late seventeenth, she had almost opted for a separate Gallican church; in the eighteenth, France had produced modern rationalism. Napoleon had treated the popes like puppets, and in the nineteenth century France had pioneered anticlericalism. The popes respected France, and feared her; their man in Paris was a key piece on the ecclesiastical chessboard.

At the beginning of 1945, the church in France was in complete disarray, and the papacy regarded with suspicion and some contempt. Roncalli's predecessor, Mgr. Valerio Valeri, had been accredited by Pius XII to the Vichy Regime, and had been kicked out of France by General de Gaulle with barely time to pack his bags. All the leaders of the Action Française, the only prewar movement in France which had received Vatican favor, were dead, in hiding, or awaiting trial and execution, or imprisonment. The main Catholic political organization, the Popular Republican Movement (MRP), had come into existence during the war not only without Vatican encouragement but in the teeth of its opposition. The French clergy, and especially the hierarchy, had been savagely divided by the civil war between the Gaullists and the Pétainists. Some of the best of the clergy were now emerging from Gestapo or Vichy prisons. Others, including bishops, were under house arrest on suspicion of collaborating with the Nazi occupying forces. When the victory of the Allies in France was celebrated in Notre Dame on 25 August 1944, the archbishop of Paris, Cardinal Suhard, had been refused permission by the authorities to be present in his own cathedral: he was *persona non grata*. His suffragan, Bishop Beaussart, was under proscription. As soon as Roncalli took up his duties he was presented with a list of thirty bishops whom the French government wished to be relieved of their offices. Many ordinary priests, whose association with Vichy had been no more flagrant, had simply been shot, often without trial.

Roncalli's instructions were to mitigate the scale of the proscriptions, if possible, and to limit the open scandal. He seems to have arrived in Paris in a state of some perturbation, a little daunted by the magnitude of his task, the splendor of his surroundings and the serious consequences for the church if he mishandled the negotiations. He kept what would now be termed a low profile and held a series of secret meetings, with the government on the one hand, and the offending clergy on the other. The archbishop of Aix-en-Provence, who had caused particular offense by a pastoral letter openly supporting Pétain, seems to have resigned of his own accord; Roncalli persuaded two others to go without fuss. With the rest, he played for time, and eventually all were allowed to continue in office. As he later put it himself, "there had been a successful attempt to strike out the nought from the number of thirty episcopal proscriptions." Among the spared was Suhard's suffragan, whom Roncalli comforted — a characteristic gesture — by making him his confessor. Part of the bargain was a display of Vatican favor to prominent anticollaborationist prelates. Roncalli secured from Rome cardinal's hats for three men who stood well with the new regime: Archbishops Saliège of Toulouse, Roques of Rennes, and de Julleville of Rouen. Roncalli was glad to oblige in this way de Gaulle himself, and Georges Bidault, leader of the MRP, who had been influential in lifting the proscriptions and was keen to have the three archbishops promoted. But he was in no doubt that it was a political bargain, as is made clear from the diaries of Jacques Dumaine (*Quai d'Orsay, 1945–51,* trans. by Alan Davidson, London, 1958), head of Protocol at the Quai d'Orsay, who became one of the nuncio's friends:

> Mgr Roncalli went on to discuss the three new French cardinals. "Their names were put forward by the government and they are fine men, so the Pope was very pleased to answer the prayers of General de Gaulle and M. Bidault — they are my strongest support. Ah, but there were difficulties. For instance, Mgr Salièges, the Archbishop of Toulouse, has been paralysed for six years and cannot utter a word, while Mgr Petit de Julleville, the Archbishop of Rouen, suffers from agoraphobia, and must always have someone with him. Only Mgr Roques is active and able to speak, so things are not very promising, are they? Your Ministers tell me that a priest should be judged by his intelligence, his priestly virtues, and his courage. I tell them that his physical presence is also important, even within the precincts of his church — and especially at his Consistory . . ."

The relations between the French government and the local episcopate continued to form by far the most important element in Roncalli's work. The witch-hunt against collaborators gradually died down, though there was a recurrence in March 1947 — the so-called *complot des soutanes* — when the police discovered that a number of wanted men had been given secret asylum in various priories and convents. Roncalli negotiated their delivery to the authorities. Much of his time was spent on securing agreement on the nomination of new bishops, about which he took a vast amount of trouble. The government had no official right to veto papal nominations; but Roncalli disclosed the proposed names, asked for comments and objections, and conveyed them to the Vatican. At the end of three years, he had successfully steered through the appointments of twenty-seven bishops, "agreed apparently without incident," as he put it, "at least as far as good relations with the authorities are concerned." For this delicate work he produced yet another of his mottoes: "*Consilium et patientia*" — take advice and show patience. The essence of ecclesiastical diplomacy, he said, "is to fear God and love men." If the Holy See, as was Pius XII's wont, worried about the long-term, he did not. If things could be kept smooth for the time being, the long-term could look after itself. He quoted a saying of Benedict XV's: "God requires us to be prudent but not to be prophets." His chief concern, as always, was that he tended to talk too much, to indulge in what Dumaine called "the nuncio's amusing chatter." "The first cardinal virtue," Roncalli told himself, "is prudence . . . it is the quintessential quality of a diplomat, so I must cultivate it with particular care. Every evening I must examine myself strictly on this point. My ready tongue often betrays me into saying too much. Beware, beware!" He kept formal, official relations to a minimum. Dumaine records:

. . . Mgr Roncalli took off his skullcap and purred: "My role in France is that of St Joseph because I discreetly

watch over and protect the interests of Our Lord. I show
myself as rarely as possible to your government, only
meeting them when they ask to see me. But M. Bidault
has reproached me for making myself too scarce, so now
we have arranged to meet once a fortnight. When Cardinal Ferrara was Nuncio at the beginning of the century, he used to visit the Quai d'Orsay every week. . . .
But in those days your ministers were usually anticlerical and the Nuncio had to remind them of his existence. I am more fortunate because I find myself among
friends whom I have no desire to embarrass."

Nine months later, in November 1946, Dumaine notes a
further encounter:

Although Mgr Roncalli is more artful than subtle, he has
had much experience and radiates a lively bonhomie.
He is at great pains not to become involved in internal
politics nor to exceed his functions as diplomatic representative of the Sovereign Pontiff. Indeed, he is well
aware of the reproach habitually cast at the Nuncio in
France, which is that of interfering with the domestic
affairs of the French clergy and of meddling in the
bishops' prerogatives . . . one of our worst faults is that
of inveigling foreigners to take part in our domestic
problems.

Evidently he avoided this pitfall: he remained on excellent terms with the episcopate. The government found
him an agreeable man to deal with, and both they, and
he, relished his little annual speeches on New Year's Eve,
when the diplomatic corps met at the Elysée Palace to
salute the President. Roncalli prepared them with great
care, and they provided splendid vehicles for his love of

aphorism. As an orator, he became surprisingly good: brief, to the point, elegant, thoughtful without being controversial; nearly all his little speeches will bear a second reading. He was evidently much attached to them. In December 1946, he had lost his voice — too much "amusing chatter"? — and his speech was read by one of his staff: "Mgr. Roncalli was distressed at losing his voice, and mimed his own speech like a deaf mute." If he was sparing in official contacts with the government, he maintained his usual policy of innumerable small gestures of friendliness. He got about a good deal and never missed a reception if he could help it. In the summer months he went on elaborate progresses through the French provinces, covering virtually all of France at one time or another, as his engagement lists show. In Lorraine he came across an episcopal tomb which gave him another motto: *Nasci, Laborare, Mori: Moderata durant.* (Roughly translated: We are born, work and die, but moderation endures.) In 1950 he went all over the French territories in North Africa. He liked to get around, be on the move; even in Paris he often escaped from his desk to go on tramps through the streets. Pius XII regarded this behavior as unsatisfactory: he was an inveterate user of the telephone, and liked his officials to be available at the other end. He commanded Roncalli to spend more time at the nunciature.

Roncalli may have found his house a little bit grand and oppressive. His Bergamesque tastes did not fit into its elaborate rococo decor. His staff was large, sophisticated, and in his opinion too uninhibited in their habit of discussing church and Vatican politics and personali-

ties. In notes he wrote during a retreat in November
1948, he contrasted their talk at table with the household
of old Bishop Radini: "there was never a single reference
to a Vatican official" that was lacking "in reverence, affection or respect"; as for women — "never a word,
never." But he decided to keep silent rather than enforce an atmosphere of constraint by issuing rebukes. He
believed in conforming to the standards of the society in
which he moved, if he could do so without sin. At first
he was a little overawed by Paris society, but he soon
fitted in, as indeed he seemed to be able to do in almost
any situation. One of his jokes went the rounds: "If a
lady turns up at a dinner party showing too much bosom,
you'd think everyone would look at her. But they look
at the Nuncio!" He gave a great many dinner parties,
and employed a first-class chef, who later opened a res-
taurant, La Grenouille, in the rue des Grands Augustins,
and related: "[Roncalli] was as fat as a curé, but he ate
like a bird. It wasn't food which swelled him out but his
books." Actually, Roncalli was worried about his weight
for most of his life, but never succeeded in doing anything effective about it. He thought that getting up very
early, at five or five-thirty, and taking long walks, would
help; he took five pieces of sugar in his coffee, instead of
six. But Paris is a notoriously weighty assignment for
diplomats. Roncalli's size never impaired his health; he
was, naturally and incorrigibly, a fat man. "I belong to
the fat man's party," he used to say when discussing
politics.

Roncalli did not make the mistake — common among
Vatican diplomats — of seeing only Catholic public men.

He was ecumenical even in politics, and cast his net as wide as he could. He became a good friend of the socialist and atheist Vincent Auriol, the president, and, still more surprisingly, of Edouard Herriot, the Speaker of the National Assembly, a Radical Socialist in the Dreyfusard tradition who had fought many bitter battles with the church between the wars. He doubtless argued that his friendship with Herriot was part of his job; in fact it was a good deal more. The two men were very much of a type, with a crackerbarrel peasant humor, so different to the mordant wit of Bidault, which Roncalli found distasteful and lacking in charity (he preferred Bidault's MRP colleague, Robert Schuman, a gentle and thoughtful Alsatian). Roncalli thought up an agreeable scheme of giving a dinner party for all the former French prime ministers still living — a considerable company. Herriot made a speech of thanks on behalf of the guests, and was moved to tears. There was another party for all the ambassadors when Dumaine was moved from Protocol to the Lisbon embassy; only the Russian, Bagolomoff, declined to come — and this was a political, not personal, gesture, for in fact Roncalli was on friendly terms with him, too. Indeed, most of the closest friendships Roncalli made in Paris were with nonbelievers, generally elderly men who had seen much of the world and, like him, had learned patience and a mixture of resignation and optimism.

There are conflicting reports on Roncalli's standing with the intellectuals both within the church and outside. His caution on public issues led many to write him off as a conservative. In a personal study, "The Roncalli

Enigma," which was published after his death by the French Jesuit Robert Rouquette in *Études*, it is claimed that he made a poor impression in Paris, and that many wrote him off as "a clown." Certainly, Roncalli was apprehensive at his ability to measure up to French cultural standards, but he did his best to get to know the intelligentsia. Dumaine describes a dinner party at the nunciature attended by, among others, François Mauriac, the great Catholic novelist, and Charles de Chambrun, another Academician: "Mgr Roncalli purrs and whirls about like a bronze and purple top." Such parties for writers and academics were frequent, and Gabriel le Bras, the famous legal historian, testified to the high level of the conversation. Roncalli found the new trends in Catholic thought which he came across in France stimulating and, occasionally, baffling. He enjoyed Father Riquet's Lenten sermons in Notre Dame on social problems. On the other hand (like a good many people) he could make little sense of Teilhard de Chardin's writings, then circulating in manuscript. It was his attitude to Teilhard which led to criticism among progressive Catholics. Father Rouquette complained that the nuncio was bewildered by Teilhard's motives, no less than by what he wrote: why did he raise so many problems, instead of contenting himself with teaching the theological and social doctrines of the church? "I underwent many labours," says Rouquette, "to make him admit that these problems were not raised by Teilhard but were raised by others, his contemporaries, and were such that he could not elude them." But if Roncalli had no sympathy for Teilhard's cast of thought, he had no animus against him either, and later, as pope, tried to disperse the cloud of suspicion which the Holy Office had cast around his published work. Indeed, Roncalli always had an affection for the outsider and the unorthodox; he used to say, "without a touch of holy madness, the church cannot grow."

As nuncio, however, Roncalli was not his own master. Pius XII allowed him very little latitude in the handling of matters of doctrinal discipline. In 1943, the pope had somewhat relaxed the fierce controls of biblical scholarship imposed during the anti-Modernist witch-hunt. But in the postwar climate of freedom which marked the late 1940s, Catholic scholars, most notably in France, took full advantage of the new atmosphere, and in the pope's view went too far. In 1950, his encyclical *Humani Generis* cracked down on the more adventurous lines of inquiry, and it was followed by the last doctrinal persecution in the history of the church. There was none of the terror which marked the anti-Modernist hunt after 1907, but a number of careers were broken. In France, men like Yves Congar, the Dominican, and Henri de Lubac, the Jesuit, were exiled to provincial houses and forbidden to publish books or articles. Roncalli had the distasteful task of passing on the orders. Not only did he dislike persecution, which he thought was almost always quite unnecessary, but he considered it absurd to try to impose restraints on biblical studies: here, once more, the church was being advised by the worst of all counselors — fear. As a matter of fact, it was Roncalli's view that the church was inclined to pay altogether too much attention to detailed points of doctrine. It was so easy to become obsessive on the subject, and fight ferocious battles over issues which the outside world found incomprehensible. Roncalli's view was doubtless prompted by the fact that he had never found theology particularly interesting. But it also reflected his knowledge, as a historian, that theological controversy — and the search for an unattainable "pure" doctrine — had in the past spent much blood to little purpose.

What did interest Roncalli were pastoral innovations. Pastoral work he regarded as the main and central activity of the church, to which all else must be subordinate. It was his chief grievance against his masters that he had been given so few opportunities to do this work himself. In the years immediately after the war, France was a theater of pastoral experiments, arising from a famous and shocking report on working-class agnosticism, *France: Pays de Mission,* which had been drawn up for Cardinal Suhard, the archbishop of Paris. The analysis was that the bulk of the working class was now so alienated from the church that it was more realistic to treat France as a mission territory rather than as the "eldest daughter." Roncalli saw in this situation the consequences of the fatal Vatican policy of cold-shouldering the Christian Democrat movements: the working class, especially in France and Italy, had been largely lost and handed over to the Communist party. Suhard's attempt to reverse the situation, by founding the so-called Mission de France, had his warm support and encouragement. From the mission sprang the limited experiment under which young priests took full-time industrial jobs (mainly in the Paris suburbs). The theory was that, only by working alongside the industrial proletariat, by being one of them,

could the new missionaries win the confidence of the
workers, in the same way that the Communist evangelists
had done. The worker-priest movement was viewed from
the outset with the greatest suspicion in Rome, and one
or two scandals — worker-priests leaving the church, or
getting married — were avidly seized on by the Holy
Office (and, it should be added, by conservative opponents in France). In August 1953, on direct orders from
Rome, the Mission de France was closed down, and the
worker-priest movement wound up. Some of the priests
in the field refused to obey these orders, and had to be
disciplined or even excommunicated. The whole affair
created much bitterness in the church.

Roncalli has been criticized by progressive Catholics
for not putting up a harder fight with Rome over the
worker-priests. In fact, his advice to Rome was to do
nothing: the experiment should be allowed to continue
until it unmistakably justified or condemned itself. This
advice seems to have been followed, for it was not until
after Roncalli had left Paris that orders were received to
abandon the mission. When he became pope, and was
urged to revive it, he preferred instead to leave it to the
council (the movement was refounded, in a much modified form, in 1965). The truth is, though Roncalli was
interested in the idea of the worker-priests, and glad the
experiment had been made, he did not think the principle was sound, or could usefully be applied, at any rate
on a large scale. His reasoning was absolutely central to
his concept of the ministry. To him, a priest was a very
special person, and a very different creature to his fellows,
someone chosen by God to perform enormously impor-

tant and highly specialized tasks. He could not be made into a worker because he was not a worker: he was a priest. Being a priest was a full-time job, because to perform his functions properly a priest needed time for prayer, for contemplation and self-examination. Roncalli had reached this view from his own experience. As a hospital orderly and sergeant he had found it impossible to lead the priestly life as he conceived it; as an officer-chaplain, he had learned to appreciate the difficulties which confronted a priest in a profane and agnostic environment. He thought it just as likely that a worker-priest would end by losing his faith, as that he would convert his workmates. Roncalli did not see the worker-priest issue as one which ought to be fought out between progressives and conservatives, and he was sorry that it had become such. To him it was a matter of practical common sense. Was this type of pastoral approach likely to bring results? On the whole, he thought not.

In retrospect, it can be argued that the worker-priest idea (as the conservatives suspected and feared) was more effective in radicalizing the clergy than in evangelizing the workers. Roncalli had no objections to a radical clergy; on the contrary. But he thought there were more effective ways of bringing this about, as indeed he proved during his pontificate.

By the end of 1952, when the worker-priest controversy was moving to its climax, Roncalli had been in Paris eight years. He was now seventy-one, still in excellent health, but conscious that everyone now classified him as an old man. Several of his brothers and sisters had died; in the autumn of 1952, he got the news that his favorite sister, Ancilla, who kept house for him during his visits to Sotto, was likely to die of stomach cancer. He looked forward to retirement, a nominal see, and a cardinal's hat: "It is the customary fate of nuncios to France," he wrote, "provided nothing goes wrong." Pius XII made him a cardinal at his end-of-year consistory, and Roncalli was delighted when President Auriol, as head of state, offered to perform the ceremony himself — an ancient privilege of the French kings. The episode, for what it was worth, was a distinct success in politico-ecclesiastical circles, where such gestures seem important, and Roncalli came in for a good many congratulations. He had to remind himself of a saying of Saint Philip Neri: "When they speak ill of you — it is true. When they pay you compliments — they're joking." Perhaps the vision of an atheist head of a secular state performing vicariously the functions of the pope brought home to Pius XII the fact that Roncalli had done an excellent job in Paris, and that there was life in the old man yet. At all events, shortly after the ceremony on 15 January 1953, he notified Roncalli that he would be leaving Paris — not for semiretirement at the Vatican, but to become patriarch of Venice. No appointment could have given Roncalli greater pleasure or sense of fulfillment.

FIVE

Pastor of Saint Mark's

WHEN RONCALLI arrived in Venice to take up his post, he had passed his seventy-second birthday. His predecessor, Cardinal Carlo Agostini, had been seven years younger at his death. Venice was clearly the end of the road for Roncalli, and a most welcome one. It was his native archiepiscopal see, and the city itself was (after Bergamo, which of course is part of the ecclesiastical province of Venice), his favorite in all the world. Soon after he arrived, he changed his will, directing that he be buried in Saint Mark's Cathedral, near the tomb of the Evangelist. He thought it would not be very long before he occupied it. There was a strain of superstition in Roncalli, as there is in nearly every Italian of peasant origins. He liked to look for evidence of coincidence, and draw conclusions. Reflecting on his appointment, he noted that Pius XI had raised another Bergamesque man, Borgo di Terzo, to the patriarchate of Venice, and that the Cardinal had then lived another six years. So perhaps he would live the same span. He noted in his diary: "I neither fear to die, nor refuse to live. . . . The span of my life — too much honoured, far beyond my merits, by the Holy See — stretches from my native village to rest among the cupolas and pinnacles of St Mark's."

But, while ready for death if it came, he accepted with considerable relish his great assignment. Though he had performed episcopal functions in Istanbul, Venice was his first opportunity to exercise to the full his pastoral capacities. "For the few years," he wrote, "that remain for me to live, *I want to be a real pastor,* in the full sense of the word." His instinct, as in diplomacy, was to get himself liked and trusted — something which never caused him much difficulty. But he thought this might not necessarily be the right course. A good pastor did not avoid controversy when the occasion demanded. He must beware of "the temptation to indulge somewhat my peace-loving temperament which is apt to make me prefer a quiet life rather than endanger myself by adopting a risky course."

The way in which Roncalli took up his duties at Venice was very characteristic of the man. He always believed in soliciting the prayers of distinguished or holy predecessors who, by any stretch of his ample historical imagination, could be considered relevant to the work before him. Thus his journey to Venice became a leisurely pilgrimage. He spent three days at Bergamo, where he prayed at the altar of Our Lady of Sorrows in Santa Maria Maggiore, over which hangs a painting of the first patriarch of Venice, Saint Laurence Justinian. He prayed to

Pius X, another patriarch of the city. Then he made a three-day retreat at the Abbey of Praglia, one of whose abbots had also become patriarch. His last stop was at Padua, where he said mass at the altar consecrated to the Blessed Gregory Barbarigo, a former bishop of Bergamo.

At Venice, he was given one of those splendid aquatic receptions for which the city is famous, and his address in reply is worth quoting in full. It illustrates perfectly his style of public speaking: that is, the way in which he conveyed important points without pretension or portentousness; the attractive combination of humility with optimism, and a manly self-confidence; above all, the simplicity, which was both deceptive and absolutely genuine:

I want to talk to you with the greatest frankness. You have waited for me impatiently. Things have been said and written about me that greatly exaggerate my merits. I humbly introduce myself.

As does any other man on earth, I come from a family and from a particular place. I have been blessed with good physical health, with sufficient good sense to see into things quickly and clearly, and with an inclination to love men, which keeps me faithful to the law of the Gospel and respectful of my own rights and of those of others. It prevents me from doing evil to anybody. It encourages me to do good to all.

I come from a modest family and was brought up in a happy and blessed poverty which has few demands, a poverty which fosters the truest and highest virtues and prepares one for the great adventure of life.

Providence took me away from my native village and led me along the roads of the East and the West. It per-

mitted me to get to know people of different religions
and ideologies, to observe grave and frightening social
problems. Yet Providence allowed me to maintain a
calm and balanced judgment. I have always been more
concerned with what unites than with what separates
and causes differences, keeping firm my belief in the
principles of the Catholic Credo and of the moral law.

And now, after this long voyage through the world,
here I am back in Venice, the land and the see my an-
cestors knew for more than four centuries. Venice —
whose history I have studied, whose people I like and
respect. I haven't the nerve to apply to my person the
words that Petrarch, that friend of Venice, said of himself, nor can I tell you wonderful tales as Marco Polo
did when he returned here. But I have my own strong
links with this place. I was born in Bergamo, the land
of St Mark, the birthplace of Bartolomeo Colleoni.
There, at the back of the hill, is Somasco, and the grotto
of St Jerome Emilien.

So, you see, I am a simple man.

The position entrusted to me in Venice is a great one.
It is beyond my merits. But I would ask you to be in-
dulgent to a man who wants simply to be your brother,
loving, approachable, understanding. I am resolved to
remain faithful to what has always been the source of
my self-respect, and which perhaps will commend itself
to you. I speak from the heart, I believe in simple manners, words and deeds, I want my sense of loyalty to be
beyond reproach.

Here, then, is the man — the new citizen of Venice
you have so kindly welcomed with such splendour.

The patriarchs of Venice have not always been popular
with the citizens, especially in modern times. Not only
the Communist party, but the anticlerical forces gener-

ally, are strong in the city. There is a great deal of heavy
industry on the outskirts, and in the island city itself
pockets of dreadful poverty amid the crumbling splen-
dors. Roncalli's predecessor had not been well liked and,
as in Istanbul and Paris, he had to begin by mending
fences. But he always took naturally to this kind of work.
To make friends with a socialist cantonal mayor, to cheer
up a discouraged parish priest, to crack jokes with the
gondoliers, to chat to the women in the fish-market —
these were things he did quite unselfconsciously and with
real pleasure. It was difficult for an anticlerical to hate a
church personified by his ample form. He was particularly courteous to committed opponents, not least journalists. He began the practice of saying an annual mass
for their intentions on 29 January, the feast of Saint
Francis de Sales, patron of writers, and one of his favor-
ites. He also, for the first time in many years, gave the
church's approval to Venice's large international colony
of artists and writers. During the last century, the patriarchs of Venice had fought a running battle with what
they supposed to be the wickedness of "Bohemia." Pius
X, when patriarch of Venice, had forbidden his clergy to
visit the Biennale, held every two years, which is probably the most important exhibition of modern painting
in the world. Roncalli had long believed that clergy,
especially in Italy, were quite pointlessly deprived of
many innocent pleasures. He thought this was one reason
why vicious clerical gossip was so common. As he noted
in his diary, reflecting on the dinner-table conversation
at the Paris nunciature, "Priests have to give up so much
— marriage, family, theatres. So many pleasures forbid-

den. So they must be allowed the greatest clerical sport —
criticism of superiors." He himself, as personal friends
testified, knew a good deal about painting. He not only
lifted the clerical ban on the Biennale, but gave a reception for visiting painters at his palace. He also arranged
for the first performance, in September 1956, of Stravinsky's *Sacred Canticle in Honour of St. Mark the Evangelist,* to take place in the cathedral itself, conducted by
the composer. When Stravinsky was in Venice, as often
happened, Roncalli liked to attend his rehearsals. The
patriarch's musical taste was conservative: Stravinsky was
about as far as he was prepared to go.

Music and painting were one thing; gambling quite
another. Roncalli hotly opposed the municipality when
it tried to move the Casino from the Lido to the center
of Venice — to the Justinian Palace, in fact. This was one
battle he won. One he lost was his attempt to resolve the
vexed question of the Iconostasis in Saint Mark's Cathedral — the marble Gothic screen which prevents most of
the congregation from seeing what is going on at the
High Altar. His proposal to remove part of it, put forward as a compromise, ran into heavy criticism, chiefly
from those who saw Saint Mark's as a monument of art
rather than a center of pastoral activity. Roncalli reacted
to what he felt was unfair comment with the "calmness"
after which he was always striving: "I am not going to
make this a polemical issue, though I think my proposal
is sound. If I were told that to get it accepted I had only
to kill a single ant, I would not kill it." The matter was
still unresolved when he left the see. Roncalli also refused
to be dragged into controversy over what clothes women

tourists were permitted to wear in the cathedral. There had been a rising volume of complaints on both sides. Roncalli's judgment was sibylline: "This is not the tropics. Nor is it the Arctic. So it is perfectly easy for women to decide what to wear."

What must be realized about Roncalli's six-year pastorate in Venice is that he was the servant of an imperious master. Pius XII took a very close interest in what was going on in the big Italian cities, and he never hesitated to interfere in detail, invariably in a conservative direction. He had no particular animus against Roncalli. A private letter he wrote to him in 1950 indicates that, in a purely personal sense, they were on reasonably courteous terms. But Roncalli came (as he put it himself) from "the other school": he was part of a progressive tradition, the tradition of Rampolla, Radini and Benedict XV, in exactly the same way that Pius was the current head of the conservative tradition. Therefore, Roncalli was not to be trusted, and there are indications that Pius supervised Venice more closely than he did certain other cities which he had confided to more dependable members of his "school." We have Roncalli's own word that he was not even consulted by Pius in the appointment of his assistant-bishop, Mgr. Augusto Gianfranceschi.

Among other things which might well have been left to Roncalli's own good judgment, the pope insisted that he hold regular retreats for the bishops of the province, and attend them personally. What is even more extraordinary, the pope appointed the "mentor." Thus, in May 1955, he dispatched to Venice the well-known Catholic broadcaster, Fr. Riccardo Lombardi S.J., who had founded an organization which Pius sponsored, the "Movement for a Better World." Lombardi specialized in preaching to mass-audiences and in giving radio talks, being variously known as "The Radio Priest" and the "Microphone of the Lord." He was not, evidently, much to the patriarch's taste; and in any case, a preacher who tuned his talks to the multitude was not, perhaps, the best choice to conduct the meditations of a select group of senior church fathers. Roncalli made no complaint, but it is significant that, as pope, he did not invite Lombardi to become one of the council's *periti,* or experts.

Pius's interference was mainly confined, however, to political matters. Roncalli was clearly under the most explicit and imperative instructions to throw the whole weight of the church in Venice against the Communists and the Socialists. Not only was he told to forbid Catholics to vote Communist; he was also obliged publicly to discountenance any electoral pacts with either branch of the Socialist party. Roncalli's own instinct was to keep the church out of politics whenever possible; a pastor's duty was to lay down general principles, but to seek to influence the voting at a local level was, in his view, improper, and likely to be unsuccessful. Nor was he happy with the pope's injunctions to give his whole-hearted support to Catholic Action, whose political efforts were sometimes intemperate and ill-calculated. But he was conscientious and loyal. He carried out Pius's instructions to the letter, even if the spirit of obedience was harder to summon. Thus, when on 9 June 1956, he addressed a meeting of the Civic Committee of Catholic Action, he made it plain that he was acting under orders, and his lackluster words have none of the rich personal flavor he liked to impart even to his minor public speeches:

> The activity of the Civic Committee is to continue: this is the directive from above. This course of action is recommended by the results of the elections which confirm the advantages of fidelity and obedience on the part of Catholics. . . . As you know, I have been at Rome, where I have been meeting with high ecclesiastical personages who carry, like your Patriarch, a heavy responsibility. We shall pursue our path in accordance with agreed directives, firm and clear. You understand me. It is necessary to remain absolutely firm, true to our principles, to our doctrine, to our faith. On the grounds of politics, or organisation, it is possible to distinguish between Communism and Socialism. In the matter of principles it is not. Communism and Socialism have the same philosophy, and they are irreconcilable with Christianity. . . . It is necessary to know how to resist a pro-Socialist outlook which is spreading even in this country, and which withers up our resources; and it is necessary to know how to resist secularism. At first sight the danger which derives from this outlook may not seem grave, but it is. And if the Pope and the bishops say it is grave they have their reasons for saying so, and the faithful ought to listen to them. This is a matter of discipline, and you understand how serious that is. Two things matter in the church: doctrine and discipline. . . . In the dangerous hour of battle and uncertainty, in an extremely delicate and difficult situation, navigation is dangerous, decision rests with the captain. Every man, therefore, to his post: let him who is to command, command, him who is to obey, obey. You have understood

me. When there is anything further to say it will be told
you at the proper time.

This very uncharacteristic utterance gives the impression of a loyal subordinate presenting a weak case in
which he clearly has no confidence.

But, while Roncalli carried out Pius's orders, he took
the risk of allowing his own personality to emerge from
time to time. When the Italian Socialist Congress met in
Venice in 1957, he insisted on publishing an address of
welcome. He made it, he said, "with respect and serenity
as a good Venetian who has a high regard for hospitality,
in accordance with the Pauline precept by virtue of which
the bishop ought to show himself *hospitalis et benignas.*"
The congress was of "exceptional importance" for "the
immediate future of our country." It was inspired "by
the desire to promote a system of understanding which
should lead to the improvement of living conditions and
to social prosperity." It was painful for him to observe
that those attending the congress professed an ideology
which did not have its origin in the Gospel. But having
made that clear, "as is becoming between courteous
friends," he hoped that the Venetians, "welcoming and
friendly as they have always been," would help to make
"this assembly of so many brothers from all parts of Italy
a profitable one, having in view a general uplifting towards the ideals of truth, goodness, justice and peace."

Given the atmosphere of Pius's last years, this was quite
a remarkable gesture. It led to head-shaking in Rome,
and may have been followed by a private rebuke, though
Roncalli was careful to base his words on the grounds of

hospitality rather than latitudinarianism. At all events, during the national elections the following year, he dutifully preached the papal line of out-and-out support for the Christian Democrats. On 9 March, in Saint Mark's, he warned the congregation: "Beware of pacts and compromises, of understandings founded upon dreams, upon promises of respect for liberty made by those who trample truth, justice, and liberty under foot without scruple." In striving to give vehemence to another man's arguments, he struck a false rhetorical note, comparing the sufferings of Pius XII — who had come under some mild personal criticism in the non-Catholic press — to the agonies of Boniface VIII at Anagni. Perhaps he feared to end his life like his old master, Bishop Radini, under a papal cloud, and in his anxiety to stand well with Pius, he said words which he must later have regretted.

The true Roncalli emerged on other occasions. He felt it natural and appropriate, as patriarch of Venice, to draw public attention to relations with the Eastern churches, on which he was admirably qualified to speak. He gave a course of lectures on the subject of Christian unity in the church hall of Saint Basso, in which he stated flatly: "The road to unity between the different Christian creeds is love, so little practised on either side." This came dangerously close to repeating one of the propositions condemned in the Syllabus of Errors, and it was certainly unfashionable at the time. Under Pius XII the church was not accustomed to admitting mistakes or shortcomings, past or present. By contrast, Roncalli asserted that the road to unity would come not through victory in argument but through magnanimity — greatness of heart,

and the spirit of loving forgiveness. After telling the story
of Joseph and his brothers, Roncalli added: "My heart is
big enough to wish to encompass all mankind." And by
all, of course, he meant all: Roncalli was not selective in
his ecumenicalism, either religious or political. He sought
not just an "opening to the left," but an "opening to the
right," in the sense that any individual came within the
orbit of his benevolence. Thus, on the twenty-fifth anniversary of the signing of the Lateran Treaty, 11 February
1954, he felt it right, in praising Pius XI's work in securing the treaty, to remind his congregation in Saint Mark's
that it was also the responsibility of another man — Mussolini, then a taboo name in Italian public speeches,
especially clerical ones. He handled the point with con-
summate tact. It was right, he said, that Mussolini should
be given the credit that was his due. Let them all "commend his soul to the mystery of the divine mercy of Our
Lord, who in the realisation of His design is accustomed
to choose the most appropriate vessels and break them
when their work is accomplished. . . . Let us respect the
fragments of the broken vessel and let us turn to good
effect the lessons they teach." Roncalli was not at all sure
he had got the tone right, and was very apprehensive
about the reception of this sermon. He was both relieved
and delighted when it raised a chorus of approval.

Roncalli's diary in Venice continues to record his quest
for "calmness, serenity." He had, to a great extent,
achieved fulfillment. He was doing the work he liked,
for which, in all honesty, he knew himself to be gifted.
He was a happy, fulfilled man, and he looked it. In the
Curia they called him, not without a slight air of con-

descension, "the good, the amiable Mgr Roncalli"; this kind of comment did not worry him — it was "the other school" talking. For a man in his mid-seventies, who had now celebrated fifty years as a priest, thirty as a bishop, he was still extremely active. He carried out a full provincial visitation of parishes, beginning it — a characteristic gesture — in the parish where his unpopular predecessor had carried out his final visit. He held a diocesan synod, on the model laid down by Radini half a century before. Roncalli took a part in local politics only at the express command of the pope; he rarely referred to national politics at all, and he took good care not to get involved in clerical controversy. But in his last years in Venice he was slowly becoming one of the best-known figures in the Italian church. With its multiplicity of splendid churches and works of art — and with the vulgarities of high society safely removed to the Lido — Venice is a favorite holiday choice for the senior Italian clergy. The hospitable Roncalli enjoyed entertaining his fellow cardinals at his palace, and also meeting and establishing friendships with cardinals from abroad, who invariably called on him when they passed through Venice, as most of them contrived to do. The old man had achieved serenity, but he was as talkative as ever. He liked to settle his guests in comfortable armchairs and have a good talk over a bottle of fine wine (he preferred the dry white wines of northeast Italy, with French champagne for special occasions). There is a touching photograph of him, taken in the rain outside Saint Mark's, with various clerics in attendance. Perhaps he is waiting for his car: at all events, he is in full spate, hands and arms in vigorous motion to drive home his words. A fat, well-adjusted, agreeable old cardinal on the threshold of eternity. Yet there was a strain of melancholy about him too, or rather the Christian apprehension which is proper to a man dedicated to divine service, who is constantly reminding himself that it is the custom of the Deity to subject even his most faithful servants to trials up to their last moments on earth. In 1957, aged seventy-six, he wrote in his diary: "I think the Lord Jesus has in store for me, before I die, for my complete mortification and purification and in order to admit me to his everlasting joy, some great suffering and affliction of body and spirit."

A year later, the trial took a quite different form to the one Roncalli had anticipated. On 9 October 1958 Pius XII died. Two days later the patriarch preached an eloquent panegyric in Saint Mark's, and then packed his bags to attend the conclave, which opened on 25 October. There was already considerable local speculation that Roncalli would be elected — voiced, evidently, in a letter he received in Rome from the bishop of Bergamo, just before the conclave began. He replied: "It matters little whether the new Pope be Bergamesque or not." But of course in this case it mattered a great deal.

SIX

The End of Isolation

THE IMPACT Pope John XXIII made upon the church and upon the world cannot really be understood except in the context of the situation he inherited. We must therefore examine, in some detail, the personality and policies of his predecessor, Pius XII. In his lifetime, Eugenio Pacelli had been regarded as one of the ablest men ever to hold high office in the church. He came from the Roman "Black Aristocracy," that is, the small, exclusive group of families who for generations have provided administrative, legal and ceremonial officials for the Vatican service. Pacelli graduated from the Pontifical Academy into the diplomatic service, and, after serving as nuncio to Germany, was made secretary of state by Pius XI. After Pius XI's death, at the conclave of February 1939, Pacelli was the overwhelming favorite to succeed. On the first ballot he got the votes of all the foreign cardinals, plus ten Italians; on the second ballot he received all but one vote. He insisted on prolonging the ceremony by calling for a third, confirmatory ballot; even so, it was the shortest conclave of modern times.

Yet Pius's long pontificate was melancholy, and in some respects a disaster for his church. The Romans loved him to the end — he was one of them — and Pius, as the first pope to exploit the resources of modern mass-communications, became a familiar figure, and voice, to millions of people throughout the world. His pale, emaciated features, the tension and concentration he radiated, gave an impression of profound spirituality: to many people, he was what a pope should look like. But those closer to him, and those who had to work with and under him, shared increasing misgivings as his reign progressed.

Pius was unlucky in that he had barely taken up his new duties as pope when the Second World War engulfed Europe. His predecessor had already issued encyclicals condemning communism, nazism and, less vehemently, Italian fascism. It ought to have been possible for Pius XII to have taken up a firm, consistent and morally defensible position towards the belligerents. In fact he never did so, and he gave the impression, later confirmed by the publication of many diplomatic documents, that he wanted Germany to win the war or at any rate survive as the dominant power in central Europe. There were two reasons for this attitude. The first was Pius's lifelong affection for all things German. He spoke the language beautifully. He had lived there many years, and some of his very few close friends, as well as his household servants, were German. He could not, or would not, or at all events did not, distinguish between the Nazi regime and the German people. He viewed with dread the prospect of a Europe in which the German state was shattered, and the German people — as he saw it — powerless to uphold Christian civilization. His second reason, of course, sprang from his fear of a German defeat: the prospect that Soviet Russia would move into the vacuum left by the collapse of German power. What he hoped to see was a German defeat of Russia followed by a peace in which the Nazis compromised with the more conservative elements in Britain and the United States.

Pius, in fact, completely misjudged the war. His hopes proved wildly unrealistic, and the Europe which emerged in 1945 confirmed his worst fears. Germany was broken; and the Communists controlled Eastern Europe, including Catholic Poland, Hungary, Czechoslovakia, Slovenia and Croatia. It was the worst disaster, in his view, that Catholicism had suffered since the end of the Wars of Religion: indeed it seemed to him to be the culmination of a tragic series of events which had begun with the Reformation. Nor was it accidental. All the evils of the modern world ultimately sprang from the repudiation of the church's authority which Martin Luther had set in motion. Pius had adumbrated this rigid and profoundly pessimistic view in his very first encyclical, published in October 1939, *Summi Pontificatus* (the English translation is under the more appropriate title, *Darkness over the Earth*). When peoples and nations chose to ignore the pope, whose authority is absolute and universal, they "did not guess what would follow, when the truth which sets us free had been exchanged for the lie which makes slaves of us. In repudiating God's law, so fatherly, so infinitely

wise, and Christ's commandments, breathing of charity,
uniting men and drawing their minds to things above,
they did not reflect that it would mean handing themselves over to a capricious ruler, the feeble and groveling
wisdom of man. They boasted of progress when they
were in fact lapsing into decadence; they conceived they
had reached the heights of achievement when they were
miserably forfeiting their human dignity; they claimed
that this century of ours was bringing maturity and completion with it, when they were being reduced to a piti-
able form of slavery."

Pius admitted that there had been disputes, even wars,
in Medieval Europe. "But," he added, "it is doubtful
whether there has ever been an age like the present, an
age in which men's spirits were so broken by despair, so
busily alive to the difficulty of providing any remedy for
their disorders. In earlier times, men had a clear consciousness of what was right and what was wrong, what
was allowable and what was forbidden. Such a consciousness made agreement easier, curbed the fierce appetites
that had been aroused, opened and paved the way for an
honourable settlement. In our day, discords arise not
merely from the violent impulses of an ungoverned temperament, but more commonly from a confusion and a
revolt in the depths of the human conscience." Thus "all
the canons of private and public honesty and decency"
had been overthrown.

Roncalli's comment on this analysis might have been
that, if Pius had known more history, he might not have
taken such a rosy view of the Middle Ages. As C. S. Lewis
once put it: "The unhistorical are usually, without know-

ing it, enslaved to a fairly recent past." Pius XII represented the culmination of the Pio Nono tradition, the
repudiation of the modern world in all its aspects, political, social and moral. In political terms this meant adamantine resistance to communism, socialism or any philosophy which, whatever its other merits, had a basis in
materialism. The church was to ally itself with conservative elements, wherever trustworthy ones were to be
found. All others were to be relentlessly opposed by
Catholic clergy and laity. Abroad, the church must ex-
hort the world to repair the injustices inflicted on Eastern
Europe in 1945. A peace without justice was not a peace.
He wrote: "A nation which is threatened by, or already
a victim of, unjust aggression, cannot remain passively
indifferent if it wishes to behave in a Christian manner
. . . the solidarity of the family of peoples forbids others
to behave as mere spectators in an attitude of passive
neutrality." Such "indifference" was wholly un-Christian.
It was never quite clear whether Pius would have given
moral support to the ideology of rollback, as it was called,
had the United States and the other Western governments put it into operation. But that was the drift of his
thinking — a capitalist-Christian crusade against Communist atheism. On the whole, he thought it was better
not to risk war: he wanted, instead, a total boycott of the
Soviet world. Thus, he had no sympathy for the United
Nations, since Russia was not only a member but on the
Security Council; the U. N. could not become "the full
and pure expression of international solidarity in peace"
until it had "cancelled from its institutions and statutes

all traces of its origin, which was rooted in the solidarity of war."

One might say that Pius, seeing his inability to create a perfect world, wanted a world which was frozen and immobile. Motion was dangerous: experience showed it invariably led in the direction of evil. Change must therefore be resisted at all costs: God, in his infinite wisdom, had condemned his church to fight a perpetual rearguard action, and every inch yielded must be bitterly contested. At the same time, while resisting change, the church must never for an instant allow her claims to be obscured and diminished. On the contrary, they must be constantly asserted in all their plenitude. Pius XII was the last of the triumphalists, bringing to its final conclusion the long history of papal claims first put forward by Hildebrand in the late eleventh century. In November 1954, in an address to a group of cardinals and bishops (printed in English as *The Authority of the Church in Temporal Matters*), he said: "The power of the church is not bound by matters strictly religious, as they say, but the whole matter of the natural law, its foundation, its interpretation, its application, so far as their moral aspects extend, are within the church's power . . ." He added: "Clergy and laity must realise that the church is fitted and authorised . . . to establish an external norm of action and conduct for matters which concern public order and which do not have their immediate origin in natural or divine law." And the source of all authority within the church was, of course, the pope.

While the claims of Pius XII, on his own behalf and that of his church, went unheeded by a great part of the world, they were enforced, so far as it was possible, among the Catholic faithful. The church of Pius still claimed to exercise control over almost every aspect of human existence, and to lay down standards of conduct in the most minute detail. So much has changed in the church since Pius's death that it is now difficult, even for Catholics, to recall the intensity of the supervision which the clergy then sought to impose on the laity, and the extent to which Catholic moral theology was still imprisoned in medieval concepts. Yet a study of works of moral theology published during Pius's pontificate — especially those issued for the guidance of confessors — quickly conjures up the moral atmosphere of those years. A characteristic volume, published in 1949, contains answers to problems submitted by confessors over a long period to the *Clergy Review*. The discussions range over an enormous number of topics, and the answers are provided in great detail. May Catholics listen to sermons, services or lectures on the radio, if given by non-Catholics? Is it obligatory, or at least permitted, for a Catholic to assist at mass celebrated by an Orthodox schismatic priest, in order to fulfill his Sunday obligation? Are women allowed to wear male dress in theatrical performances? Which types of modern dances were liable to be a proximate, or remote, occasion of sin? What minimum sum of money constituted mortal sin in cases of theft? (Answer: $15, and twice as much for children and members of religious orders.) Is knitting servile work, to be forbidden on Sunday? Is the use of dripping and suet forbidden on days of abstinence? What are the rules regulating the practice of genuflecting on the part of the faithful when they kiss a bishop's ring? Naturally, many of the most complex questions, leading to the most elaborate answers, centered around sexual morality and birth control. What is the state of theological opinion on the lawfulness of excising a cancerous womb containing an unviable fetus? Is a chemist's assistant allowed to continue working in a shop at which she knows contraceptives are sold? Can a wife use a vaginal lotion when she knows her husband has venereal disease? Since venereal disease is a disincentive to sexual misconduct, is it lawful to support VD clinics? What precisely may a woman use in the form of medical and hygienic aids during a menstrual period? May a confessor interrogate, on the subject of their marriage relations, all married penitents in a district where the practice of contraception has reached alarming proportions? What, for the purposes of diagnosing sin, is an exact definition of sexual pleasure? (Answer: "It is an operation which begins with the first typical excitation of the genitals — that is, with the function of the erectile nerves and the turgescence of the organs, and if this organic change is present together with any of the psychic elements of passion there is what the theologians call *delectatio venerea* . . . for the last three centuries it has been the common teaching that it does not admit smallness of matter" — that is, venial sin.)

The church of Pius XII claimed to have the answers to all problems, and Pius, as its authoritarian ruler, made it his personal business to familiarize himself with as many aspects of human existence as possible. In a sense he tried to become the universal man. In addition to Latin and Italian, he spoke English, French, German, Spanish and Portuguese fluently, and he could deliver speeches in Danish, Dutch, Swedish and other languages. He believed that the pope had to give exact moral guidance to men and women of every profession and calling in life. Hence, he was a voracious reader of technical manuals, and he could discourse, with an appearance of expertise, on a vast number of subjects: medicine and dentistry, architecture, heating engineering, chemistry, public health, acting, journalism, printing, the law, diesel engines, aeronautics, celestial navigation, radio engineering: the list is endless, and Pius was constantly adding to the number of specialist subjects on which he was prepared to make speeches. He seems to have believed that the best way to establish a rapport with people was to learn the technology of their profession, and much of his time was spent receiving delegations of professional bodies, to whom he spoke in eloquent detail on the nature and difficulties of their work. His encyclicals, and published letters and speeches, cover a vast range of subjects, usually in considerable technical detail. Pius was a passionate film fan — Hollywood stars were always welcome visitors at the Vatican in his day — and one of his last encyclicals, *Miranda prorsus* (1957), dealt with the cinema, sound broadcasting and TV, in a way which was typical of his methods. He did not hesitate to lay down in detail the duties of a news announcer; the way in which regional censorship offices should be set up and operated; the moral responsibilities of cinema managers, distributors, and actors; the duty of bishops to rebuke erring Catholic cinema directors and producers, and if necessary to impose appropriate sanctions on them; the obligation of Catholic

members of festival juries to vote for "morally praise-
worthy" films; and even the criteria by which posters ad-
vertising movies were to be judged.

This vast output of technical advice on a growing
number of subjects makes curious reading today. Of
course, being concerned with details, it got out of date
very rapidly; the professional people were flattered by
Pius's interest in their *arcana,* but not on the whole im-
pressed by his knowledge, which was necessarily super-
ficial, or inclined to take his advice. As an exercise in
public relations, it had its merits; otherwise, it was very
largely a waste of time. And it consumed so much of
Pius's energies that little was left for the administration
of the church. Increasingly, as he grew older, Pius reduced his contacts with the Curia. It became very difficult
for the cardinals who headed the various congregations,
or ministries at the Vatican, to get an appointment with
him. He gave his orders over his white-and-gold telephone: he phoned direct, without using a secretary, and
when officials heard his voice — powerful, rather nasal —
they used to go down on their knees with the phone in
their hands. Pius was prepared to take on any amount of
public appearances — no pope has given so many public
or semipublic audiences. What he disliked more and
more were business meetings, where facts he found un-
congenial might be presented to him, and where he might
be faced with argument or even opposition. He behaved
like an absolute monarch of the *ancien régime,* and an
increasingly isolated one. All but the most privileged and
senior officials addressed him on their knees, and left the
room walking backwards. Like Queen Victoria, Pius

could not bear to be seen (or to see people) when out walking, and the gardeners and other staff had instructions to hide behind trees if they came across the pope in the Vatican gardens — which were then tightly closed to all but a select few. Pius invariably ate his meals alone, not even his favorite relatives being allowed to sit down at table with him. An exception was made for Cardinal Spellman of New York, who was usually invited to take tea with the pope whenever he arrived in Rome. Spellman was acceptable to Pius, not only because he was highly successful in raising money, and handled the Vatican's Wall Street portfolio, but because he indulged the pope's taste for the latest mechanical gadgets. It was Spellman who gave him his white typewriter and his white-and-gold electric razor; and it was Spellman who presented the papal Cadillac, which had solid gold door-handles and, in the back, a single seat where the pope sat in solitary splendor.

Spellman was the only member of the Sacred College to whom Pius showed any personal favor. The three most important curialists were Cardinals Canali, Ottaviani and Pizzardo, who formed part of what was known as "the Pentagon," a group of five which ran the Vatican state and the central organs of the church. Curiously enough, Pius rarely saw the three cardinals, especially in his last years: the two lay members of the Pentagon, his nephew, Prince Carlo Pacelli, and the Vatican architect, Enrico Galeazzi, had much greater access to him. Pius had a very serious illness in 1954 and, though he recovered, his eccentricities became much more pronounced in the last years of his life, and his style of government more Byzantine and weird. He had seen his first "visions" on three consecutive days in the autumn of 1950, but after his illness his belief in personal miracles became more insistent and their occurrence more frequent. In the last four years of his life he rarely saw the heads of the government departments, though he occasionally phoned them: they would hear *"Qui parla Pacelli* [Pacelli speaking]," followed by a long recital of grievances, reproaches or instructions, and then the pope would hang up before they had a chance to reply or explain.

Pius was his own secretary of state. For many years the routine duties were performed jointly by two archbishops, Monsignors Tardini and Montini; but Pius declined to give either the formal title. Nor would he give them cardinal's hats. At one point he claimed that he had offered to make both cardinals, but both had declined from a sense of humility and unworthiness, a most improbable tale. What is conceivable is that Tardini declined in order to make it impossible for Montini (whom he feared would succeed if Pius died) to accept. Or Pius may have invented the story. Following a row with Montini he moved him away from the Curia to the archbishopric of Milan; but, against all precedent, he refused to raise him to the cardinalate, which in effect meant that Montini had no chance of succeeding him; there can be little doubt that this omission was deliberate. That left Tardini to supervise the old pope by himself, and there is no doubt that he found it hard going. In 1960, with Pius safely in his grave, he published a malicious little sketch of Pius and his methods of work, including this description of the way he signed a routine document:

He used very fine pen nibs. The ink had to be always
very black. After having carefully smoothed out on his
desk the paper he was going to sign, the Pope, with a
calm and, I would say, loving gesture, picked up with
his right hand the pen, which was always on the same
place on his desk. Then he carefully scrutinised the nib
to make sure there was no minute thread or some other
impurity which might make the writing too thick. If he
saw anything of the kind, or even if he merely suspected
there could be, he took a little black cloth (which also
was always in the same place on his desk), and carefully
cleaned the nib. After having made sure that everything
was in order he laid down the pen — this time alongside the sheet of paper he was going to sign — and, very
slowly, pulled up the right-hand sleeve of his white
soutane. Then he seized the pen with the thumb, the
index and the middle fingers of his right hand and, extending the arm, he lifted with the other two fingers the
lid of the inkpot. This was an old-fashioned affair, and
the lid was always kept shut to prevent dust falling in the
ink. After that, the Pope dipped the point of the nib in
the inkpot with great care to prevent it from collecting
too much ink, and soiling the desk or the paper. At
last the Holy Father started to write his signature. He
wrote calmly, very slowly, taking care that the ink
should come out thicker in some places and thinner in
others, to produce an effect of *chiaroscuro*. He ended his
signature with a flourish, which completed this painstak-
ing piece of work. Then he carefully wiped the nib with
the piece of black cloth, to make sure that no trace of
ink was left; "otherwise," he said, "the nib gets rusty
and cannot be used again." Then he replaced the pen
and the cloth in their proper places. Finally, he handed
the signed document to the person who had been waiting for it, invariably cautioning him to wait before
placing it among other papers, so that the ink would

have time to dry and there would be no risk of the signature being smudged.

There is no doubt that Pius became very odd in his
last years. His own interests were increasingly medical,
or paramedical. Among his intimates was the conservative
Catholic Action leader, Professor Luigi Gedda, a doctor
who specialized in the physiology and psychology of twins.
Pius made friends with, and patronized, the Swiss Dr.
Paul Neihans, who gave him hormone injections, and
who was made a member of the Pontifical Academy of
Science in 1955. A third medical friend was his own personal physician, Riccardo Galeazzi Lisi, the half brother
of the architect Enrico Galeazzi. The Galeazzi connec-
tion, and Pius's relations with his three nephews, especially Prince Carlo (all were awarded their titles by the
Italian state, as a courtesy to the pope) led to charges of
nepotism. There does not seem to have been any direct
element of corruption in the Pius regime, but the nephews, and Enrico Galeazzi, held a number of important
financial posts and directorships both within and without
the Vatican, which have been explored in considerable
detail in Corrado Pallenberg's book, *The Vatican Finances,* published in 1971. They undoubtedly owed their
rise and prominence to Pius's favor; but Enrico Galeazzi,
at least, appears to have done his work — he was, in effect, the governor of the Vatican state — with considerable success, and was retained in his post for a decade
after Pius's death. What dismayed many Catholics was
not only the personal and family element in the pope's
appointments but the fact that the men he selected were

so closely identified with the world of high finance, which thus seemed to receive the stamp of the pope's approval.

The remainder of Pius's inner circle was made up of "the Germans." Some were of outstanding quality. His personal confessor, the Jesuit Cardinal Augustin Bea, was to play a remarkable role under John XXIII. Another friend, Mgr. Ludwig Kass, had formerly been a leader of the German Center party, had fled from Hitler to Rome, and had there entered the priesthood. Pius was also well served by two German personal secretaries. What did arouse resentment, however, was the influence of his Bavarian housekeeper, Mother Pasqualina Lehnert, which continued to grow until his death. This nun, who had been born in 1894, belonged to a German order which specialized in training women for domestic service in clerical households. She had worked in a recuperation center for sick priests in Switzerland, where Pius, then a young Vatican diplomat, had met her. In 1917, he brought her to Munich, where he was nuncio, to keep house for him, and from then on she took charge of the domestic side of his life. She not only supervised the kitchen and the maids but made herself personally responsible for his health and well-being: Pius was one of the delicate types who are always verging on valetudinarianism, but who contrive to live to an advanced age. Her importance in his life is demonstrated by the fact that, during the papal conclave of 1939, she was allowed to remain with him, to attend to his needs, within the sealed area — the only recorded instance of a woman being granted this privilege.

After Pius was elected pope, her power became formidable. She has been described as "short-tempered, despotic,

frightfully outspoken"; the three German nuns, who provided the maid-service for the papal apartments, were
terrified of her, and she was allowed to overrule the papal
butler, Signor Stefanori. Outside the Vatican walls, indeed outside Pius's own quarters, she was rarely seen, and
was never photographed except by a long-range camera.
In public, she effaced herself; but in private she was authoritative. During his last years, Pius suffered from acute
arthritis, and was often unable to write: he formed the
habit of dictating to Mother Pasqualina — not only state
papers but his private diary. No doubt his motive in using
her in this way was that he could rely absolutely on her
discretion; and this was justified in that, after his death,
her lips remained firmly sealed. But their relationship
inevitably allowed her to influence the pope on matters
well beyond her province. It was said that she determined
certain matters of high policy, and even secured the appointment of a cardinal, Lèger of Montreal. These stories
were doubtless exaggerated in the atmosphere of resentment she aroused in the Curia. But what could not be
denied was that her close supervision of the pope's health
and comfort allowed her, in practice, to determine who
could, or could not, get to see Pius for a private talk. She
was thus, in a sense, an unofficial vizier, and men of great
weight in the church, even cardinals, found it necessary
to pay court to her.

The tragedy of Pius's decline is that the stifling and
unseemly atmosphere of his court began to affect the
church as a whole. Decisions were delayed, or taken in
secret, often behind the backs of responsible officials.
There was a widening chasm between the papal apart-

ments, where all power ultimately resided, and the Curia itself. In many respects, they operated as two separate governments, sometimes in conflict. Though Pius took all the decisions in some spheres, down to the smallest details, in others the Curia was given free rein, and worked on, in its own bureaucratic manner, stifling initiative and strengthening its grip on the routines of the church everywhere. Bishops and cardinals throughout the world, responsible for vast congregations, faced with problems of great urgency, found that they could not obtain access to the pope when they visited Rome, and were forced to make their own separate deals with Curia officials. There was a feeling, during these years, that the church was almost entirely stagnant, a great machine running down for lack of a vital controlling force. Pius had always seen the church as a beleaguered citadel: at the end of his life it became one, in more than a notional sense, but a citadel crumbling from within, manned by a garrison without officers, and with commander increasingly divorced from reality. Pius, wrote Guiselle Dalla Torre, former editor of the official Vatican paper, *L'Osservatore Romano,* "separated himself from direct contact with life, though not, unfortunately, from people who abused his confidence." His own interests became increasingly pietistic and credulous. He was obsessed by the prophecies of the Fatima-miracle children, by the prodigies worked by the Bavarian girl Theresa Neumann, and by his own mystic visions and dreams, some of which were leaked to the press. Some prelates feared he might suddenly announce a new and controversial dogma: there were rumors, for instance, that he planned to declare the Virgin Mary to be the co-redemptress, and thus plunge the church into mariolatry. In his old age, the great organization he controlled seemed to have lost any semblance of intellectual virility, any sense of pastoral mission, any desire to come to grips with the problems of the real world, and to be settling into a childish, devotional dotage. The church appeared to be dying with him.

Pius's actual death, though edifying, brought the scandals to a head. During his last few days, his doctor, Galeazzi Lisi, kept a diary, and he gave this to the press within days of the pope's death. He wrote an article for the French weekly, *Paris-Match,* and this was, apparently, accompanied by photographs he had taken while Pius was *in extremis.* There was wild bidding among newspapers and agencies for sensational copy and photographs of the deathbed scenes, and photographers and TV cameras were allowed into his bedroom within minutes of the doctor's certifying that life was extinct. Pius himself had exploited the media of mass-communication: now, they took their revenge. To make matters worse, Galeazzi Lisi attempted a new method for preserving the pope's body. He was not content with the normal procedure, in which embalming followed the removal of the internal organs, but believed he had rediscovered the so-called Egyptian Method, in which the body was preserved intact. The experiment was a failure (the doctor called a press conference to explain why). As one observer recorded: "Decomposition was obvious even before the lying-in-state in St Peter's was over, despite repeated efforts to give a more wholesome appearance to the decaying remains. Members of the Noble Guard are said to have fainted at their posts." In a superstitious city like Rome, where it was confidently expected that Pius would soon be canonized, and where the absence of putrefaction is popularly supposed to be a test of sanctity, the shock and anger were intense. Cardinal Tisserant, as dean of the Sacred College, took over the central administration immediately after the pope's death, until the election of a successor. He moved swiftly to repair the damage, and within days most of the members of Pius's personal coterie had packed their bags and left. Among them was Mother Pasqualina, who returned to Germany in secrecy and silence.

But more fundamental measures were required. It was easy enough to open the windows of the papal apartments, and disperse the fetid atmosphere which had gathered there. What was required was to open the church as a whole to the world. It was this need which essentially conditioned the conclave of 1958, and determined its outcome. Virtually all the cardinals who assembled in Rome in the fortnight before 25 October 1958, when the conclave began, were dissatisfied with the government of the church, though in different degrees, and for different reasons. Most of those who came from abroad wanted a more outward-looking church, and therefore a pope who would bring it about. Most of the Curia cardinals wanted a pope who would associate himself fully and regularly with the central government of the church. The remaining Italian cardinals wanted a man of experience and wisdom, who would accommodate these two (not necessarily conflicting) demands without unleashing irresistible forces of change. They all knew they were taking an important decision: this was not an ordinary papal election.

Characteristically, with his minute attention to detail, Pius XII, as long ago as 1945, had revised and updated the rules for conducting a conclave, in his Apostolic Constitution, *Vacantis Apostolicae Sedis*. He had set out the procedure exactly, and instructed that a papal chamberlain, and other officials, be charged with its observance. But, equally characteristically, he had failed to appoint a chamberlain. The cardinals thus had a full voting process, and no presiding officer. There were other mishaps. By tradition, the conclave, which is cut off from the outside world to prevent any attempt to influence its deliberations, communicates only by smoke, which appears from an old iron chimney jutting up from the roof of the Sistine Chapel, the heart of the conclave. Ballots take place twice a day. It is commonly supposed that, if the ballot is inconclusive, the smoke is black; if a pope has been elected, it is white. In fact, what happens is that, when an inconclusive ballot has been held, the discarded voting slips are burned with a mass of damp straw, and the smoke (usually black) comes out in considerable quantity. If the ballot is successful, the slips are burned without straw: the smoke is then thin, wispy, grayish. Before the 1958 conclave, it was found that the Sistine Chapel stove had disappeared — possibly sold as a relic. A new one was produced, and this, added to the fact that very few of those present had attended a previous conclave, led to a breakdown in the smoke-signals. It was impossible for the thousands of those waiting in Saint Peter's Square to judge, from the color and quantity of the smoke, whether a pope had been elected or not, as each combustion took place. After John XXIII had been elected, he amended the Apostolic Constitution to provide for a clear system of signals; and he also imposed, under pain of excommunication, a ban on photographs of a dying pope.

Cardinal Roncalli of Venice arrived in Rome some ten days before the conclave was due to begin, staying at the Domus Mariae on the Via Aurelia. On Sunday, 25 October, early in the afternoon, he entered Saint Peter's in procession with the fifty other cardinals, and then proceeded to the Vatican Palace, the conclave area being sealed off and guarded. He was lodged in the Noble Guard wing of the palace, along with the archbishops of Saragossa, Palermo, Quito and Buenos Aires, and the Vatican Prefect of Rites. One of his best-informed biographers, Meriel Trevor, states that his name was "not high on the list of *papabile* drawn up by the gambling Romans for the Totopapa." This is not correct: the volume of betting in Milan, at least, made him the favorite, at odds varying between three and five to one.* Roncalli's

---

* After the beginning of the conclave, Roncalli was quoted at two to one; there were odds of three to one on Cardinals Ottaviani and Agagianian, five to one on Tisserant and Ruffini, and six to one on Siri and the Polish cardinal, Wyszynski. Betting on the outcome of a papal conclave is, of course, an offense punishable by excommunication. Among the journalists attending the conclave, Roncalli was judged, on balance, to be the most likely winner: so I reported to the British Sunday newspapers, *Reynolds News*, immediately before the conclave began. It was also clear, at any rate to me (and I was by no means alone) that Roncalli's election would introduce an era of change in the church. Immediately after his election, I published an article, "Rome Goes Left," in the French weekly magazine, *L'Express*, and in the British weekly, the *New Statesman*, indicating the radical form these changes would take. This was not well received in many Catholic quarters. In Paris, the celebrated French novelist François Mauriac, who then wrote a weekly diary published on the back page of *L'Express*, objected strongly to the publication

secretary, Monsignor Capovilla, later recorded that from the outset of the conclave the patriarch was accorded what he terms "delicate attentions" by a number of cardinals, both Italian and foreign. Roncalli's only known comment on the voting was written just before the opening of the council in 1962, and forms one of the last entries in his journal, entitled: "Summary of great graces bestowed on a man who thinks poorly of himself." He writes: "To have accepted with simplicity the honour and burden of the pontificate, with the joy of being able to say that I did nothing to obtain it, absolutely nothing; indeed, I was most careful and conscientious to avoid anything which might direct attention to myself. As the voting in the conclave wavered to and fro, I rejoiced when I saw the chances of my being elected diminishing and the likelihood of other, in my opinion truly most worthy and venerable persons, being chosen." Roncalli's own vote, according to Vittorio Gorresio, a leading papal commentator of the time, was given (with a characteristic delicacy of touch) to the man he had superseded in Paris, Valerio Valeri.

The secrets of this particular conclave have not yet been divulged by anyone in a position to know them; all that we can say for sure is that Roncalli was chosen at the eleventh ballot, on the afternoon of Wednesday October

---

of my article, and was with difficulty persuaded from resigning from the paper. In Britain, the appearance of my article in the *New Statesman* aroused many protests from Catholics, including one addressed privately to myself (in the form of a postcard) from the Catholic novelist Evelyn Waugh. It read: "I see your vision of the future Church: coloured cardinals distributing contraceptives to the faithful." The article is reprinted in my volume of collected essays, *Statesmen and Nations* (London 1971).

28. But it is fairly clear that he received a substantial total on the first ballot, and that the subsequent balloting, while not pushing him over the top of the two-thirds-plus-one majority required (this extra vote had been made mandatory by Pius XII, to prevent any cardinal's vote being decisive in his own election), made it clear both that a large, mixed group of cardinals would have him and no one else, and, secondly, that no other candidate was acceptable to them. When this became clear beyond any possibility of misunderstanding, on the Tuesday, Roncalli began to get the extra votes needed. The truth seems to have been that Roncalli, from the outset, had the support of a number of Italian noncurial cardinals, who liked and respected him; of the French cardinals, who believed he was sympathetic towards their country and its problems, who thought, in some cases, that they owed their hats to him, and who formed the largest block after the Italians; and of Cardinal Tisserant, who was able to influence the voting of several Curia cardinals. In many respects, Roncalli was excellently placed. He had been closely associated with the international work of the church without at any point in his career being, strictly speaking, part of the Curia establishment. This stigma was, indeed, fatal to the chances of Cardinals Aloisi Masella and Agagianian, who in other respects were strongly favored. What is more, Roncalli was known to be in the tradition of Benedict XV, a supporter of a moderately liberal approach. He was credited with certain views of a reformist nature; he was also judged to be a man who had never been an avowed partisan, who had made no enemies, who had leaned over backwards to conciliate

those from "the other school," and who could be relied upon to conduct any indispensable changes within an atmosphere of friendliness and calm. It is thus untrue to say, as some believed at the time, that he was chosen as a "stop-gap pope," an old man who could hold the fort for a year or two until the balance of forces within the church became clearer. On the contrary: he was elected with a definite, if modest, mandate for change. But what clinched his election, especially in the final stages, was his personal qualities: his modesty, his courtesy and diffidence, his evident warmth and decency, above all his long record of conspicuous loyalty to the Holy See. A majority, and eventually a large majority, of the cardinals came to the conclusion that he would make not only the kind of pope they felt was needed, but a good pope, *tout court*.

Roncalli's acceptance of the papacy was very much in character. He noted that he had been elected on the feast of Saints Simon and Jude, Saint Jude being the patron of lost causes. When Tisserant, as dean, asked him, according to the formulary, by what pontifical name he would be known, he answered: *"Vocabur Johannes."* Then he read from a scrap of paper he had prepared: "The name John is dear to me because it is the name of my father. It is dear because it is the title of the humble parish church where we received baptism." More popes, he added, had been called John than by any other name — thus brushing aside the fact that John XXII had been a failure, and that the title of John XXIII had already been usurped by a schismatic antipope. He pointed out that nearly all his Johannine predecessors had had a brief pontificate. John was also the name of the Baptist, "the unconquered wit-o

ness of truth, of justice, and of liberty in preaching," and of the disciple and evangelist, "who had leaned on the breast of Our Lord at the Last Supper." He trusted that both would "plead for our most humble pastoral ministry." Meanwhile, he said to the cardinals: "My children, love one another. Love one another, because that is the greatest commandment of the Lord." It was a typical little sermon of the Roncalli stamp, simple yet subtle, inoffensive yet pregnant. Then he put on his new white skullcap, placing his discarded red one on the head of Monsignor di Jorio, the secretary to the conclave, thereby signifying that he raised him to the cardinalate: a revival of the kind of innocent old custom which he found delightful.

But his first act of state was totally unexpected. He commanded the cardinals to remain in conclave with him for a further twenty-four hours, so that he would have the chance to consult with them. The cardinals, no doubt, were anxious to get out of their confined quarters (many of them were very old indeed — one was ninety-six — and several were ailing). But they accepted the command in the spirit in which it was given: John's eager desire to draw all of them into the government of the church, in striking contrast to his predecessor. It was an augury of things to come. But the command, naturally, was not at once communicated to the outside world. The announcement of the new pontiff was made at four forty-five, from the balcony of Saint Peter's. Tardini, the acting secretary of state, assumed that the conclave was now over and, together with a cluster of senior officials, burst into the sealed area to make his mark with his new master. This aroused the righteous anger of Tisserant, who excommunicated Tardini on the spot — the canonical punishment for interrupting a conclave. It was a bizarre episode, half-comic, half-serious. No one could recall the last occasion on which a secretary of state, even an acting one, had been cut off from the church. Pope John, in great good humor, lifted the penalty the next day. But it was, all the same, the first sign, and a disturbing one, to the monsignori of the Curia that the church had entered a new age.

SEVEN

Opening Windows

THE POPES OF MODERN TIMES have varied enormously in personality: Pius IX, volatile, vain and emotional; Leo XIII, the diplomat with the grand manner and the imperious phrase; Pius X, the handsome giant with the bitter conservatism of the successful peasant; Benedict XV, shy, crippled, gentle and perceptive; Pius XI, the dull bourgeois pedant, who grew more sharp and interesting as he aged; Pius XII, the solitary ascetic and polymath, feline and dictatorial. Yet their characters tend to be merged in the anonymous solemnity of their office, the unquestioning veneration with which they are surrounded, the stereotyped *pietas* with which they are presented by the ecclesiastical apparatus to the hundreds of millions of Catholics throughout the world. They become blurred: holy men dressed in white, remote from the world, distant figures, their arms raised in the rituals of their craft, seen across the heads of tumultuous, cheering

crowds. Their acts and writings, too, justified and ho-
mogenized by the machinery of propaganda, encrusted,
as they always are, by references to precedents and their
predecessors, couched in the formal language of state
documents, appear depersonalized and uniform in tone.
Only the insiders are capable, at the time, of judging the
nuances of papal statesmanship; the real significance of
a pontificate is often understood, if at all, only after —
sometimes long after — the subject is dead.

It is remarkable that John XXIII, almost from his
very first day in office, broke through this carapace of
anonymity, and emerged as a vivid human being, with
instantly recognizable characteristics, and with a marked
bent of policy. He was not the pope: he was "Pope John."
Much of this impact, of course, was due to the activities
of the news media, who were quick to grasp that they had
struck a rich vein of material. Much was due, also, to the
almost total contrast with John's predecessor, who had
been largely inaccessible in his last years, except at formal
audiences. There was, too, the element of agreeable surprise, almost shock, when it was discovered that the newly
elected pope, whom the world saw as a very old man,
chosen to keep his office ticking over until new forces in
the church made their appearance, flatly declined to
accept his passive role, and plunged energetically into the
thick of things. When all this is said, however, it was
essentially the personality of the man himself which
brought about the change. It was as though the whole
of his life and experience had prepared him for this
moment, had slowly assembled within him the elements
of a natural ruler, who was waiting to be unleashed.

When the task was finally presented to him — aged seventy-six, almost seventy-seven — he had no hesitations, no doubts. He simply did what, unconsciously, he had been training himself to do since he first became a priest: he spoke and acted as a wise pastor, but from the universal vantage point of the papal throne. This, indeed, is what Christianity is about; it is what the papacy should be about, and so rarely is. The people responded, very quickly: they recognized that here was not a product of public relations, or of calculation and policy, but an absolutely genuine article. John was being himself.

It is important to grasp that John was a product both of experience and of self-experience. In some respects the latter was much more important in explaining his papacy. His career had brought him into contact with vast numbers of people who needed to be handled with finesse, and a wide range of situations which required tact and intelligence. He had learned to be a diplomat in the best and broadest sense, and this background undoubtedly proved of great value when he assumed the papacy. But there was also the inner struggle, reflected in his diary, which had been progressing throughout this time. Without being in any way neurotically introspective, John had a lifetime's habit of looking at himself steadily; he learned to be honest with himself. He did not, except in a notional sense, seek perfection: what he tried to do was to build on his natural qualities and emerge, year by year, a better and more useful person. He tried to curb his ebullience without killing it; to achieve a state of calm which was not soporific, but reflective and therefore creative. It was as though he had found himself a rough-hewn block of sound marble, and had spent his life chiseling it into shape. The essence of the spiritual life is the quest for balance. The object, goodness, is clear enough. The difficulty lies in steering towards it between the rival rocks of despair and pride. The human soul must retain its sense of humility and fear of failure, without at the same time denying itself the creative encouragement of success. John never put this problem into precise words: but it underlies many entries in his diary, and one feels that he was nearing the point of balance during his years as patriarch of Venice. The result was that he became, in all humility, a confident man, with a confidence based not on ignorance, but on self-knowledge. Then, on becoming pope, his confidence was further strengthened by his simple moral theology. As a subordinate, internal peace was to be found through obedience. But obedience, in the larger sense, meant submission to Providence. Providence had made him pope; he had not sought the place — it had been given him, in the full knowledge of his qualities and frailties. He would, therefore, obey Providence, by doing what he felt to be right, and Divine Providence would protect him from error. He believed in the inspiration of God in all things, but especially in his capacity as pontiff: not, as it were, in sudden, blinding flashes of illumination, nor in the sense that he could communicate directly with the Deity and ask for instructions; but in the deeper sense that God had created and shaped him for certain purposes, and therefore endowed him with instincts and habits of thought which were trustworthy. He wrote in his journal in 1959: "This is the mystery of my life. Do not look for other explanations. I have always repeated Saint Gregory Nazianzus's words: 'The will of God is our peace.' " Now it was God's desire that he should be pope, and follow his bent.

John expressed his serenity as a ruler on innumerable occasions. He was crowned on November 4, a week after his election, happily choosing the feast day of one of the saints he admired most, Saint Charles Borromeo. His coronation speech was brevity and simplicity itself: he wished to be a pastoral pope, and in doing so would submit himself fully to his Divine Master. Afterwards, he was carried into the Hall of Benedictions on the *Gesta Sediatoria,* and addressed a group of people from his own part of Italy. John had no love for the *Gesta,* an antique machine of ceremonial symbolism which links the papacy to the days of imperial Rome, and emphasizes the pontiff's claims to a temporal power which has fortunately vanished. He thought it absurd, and quite possibly dangerous, too. It made him seem, and feel, a freak. But he turned the incongruity of his position into a felicitous image. "Here we are again," he said, "on a new journey. Here we are, carried high by our children." Seventy years ago, he had first come to Saint Peter's, carried on his father's shoulders. Those seventy years had been happy because, by the grace of God, he had been able to devote them to divine service: "The secret of all this is to let oneself be carried by the Lord, and to carry him."

It was as a man carried by the Lord that John entered his pontificate. The speed with which he acted made it clear that he was in no doubt of the direction he wished to travel. His fundamental decision to call an Ecumenical

Council seems to have been taken, according to Monsignor Capovilla, almost immediately after his election. He was an old man in a hurry, but an old man moving with all deliberate speed. He was not one to ponder long before making up his mind, or to agonize after he had issued his orders. As one Vatican official remarked: "He seems to have been pope all his life." There is good reason to believe that John deliberately helped to popularize the view that he was a man free, if not from anxieties, at any rate from nagging worries. He was anxious that his own confidence in Providence should be shared. It was part of his plan to generate a new spirit of optimism in the church. Let the faithful feel that they were under the guidance of a man who was not continually fussing over the maps and compasses, and changing the route. Hence the little stories he told about himself which, as he knew very well, would be quickly publicized and relished. Thus he related that, in his first weeks as pope, he was kept awake by a problem. "I said to myself: 'I will ask the Pope about it.' Then I remembered: 'But *I* am the Pope.' So I said to myself: 'Right, I will ask God about it.'" If he couldn't sleep, he told friends, he used to say: "Don't take yourself so seriously, Angelo." But, he added, he nearly always slept well, usually from ten to four in the morning, when he got up to start work again. When he took off his white skullcap at night, he would say to it (he claimed): "Lie there pope, now I must sleep." These anecdotes, indicating John's easy physical adjustment to his job, did their work. Indeed, as always happens in such cases, the genuine stories bred apocryphal ones, making the same point. Thus, in the

Second World War, during the darkest period of Britain's isolation, tales of Churchill's extraordinary ability to drop off to sleep without effort or worry, whenever he had a spare hour or so, bred reassurance in a frightened people (though the later publication of his doctor's diaries show that, in fact, he often relied heavily on sleeping pills).

The Johannine anecdotage in fact reflected the truth: the presence on the papal throne of a man who was not fearful. John knew and loved the Gospel intimately, and unlike many recent popes, he frequently quoted it. Jean Guitton has recorded an episode one evening at Castel Gandolfo, the pope's summer residence. John pointed to the silver cupola of the papal observatory, standing out against the blackness of the sky, and said: "You see, these learned astronomers make use of the most complicated apparatus to guide men. I know nothing about such things. Like Abraham, I content myself with advancing through my night step by step, by the light of the stars." On another occasion, in the Vatican gardens, watching the setting sun turn Michelangelo's great dome of Saint Peter's into a parabola of blazing light, he quoted to Monsignor Capovilla a passage from Saint John Chrysostom:

> Christ has left us on earth to become beacons that give light, teachers who give knowledge. So that we may discharge our duty like angels, like heralds among men. So that we might be grown men among the young, men of the spirit among men of the flesh, and win them over; so that we might be seed, and produce many fruits.

John repeatedly spoke of what he termed "the simple, God-fearing man," a concept often referred to in the Old and New Testaments, which he took to be the archetype of the true Christian. In August 1961, at Castel Gandolfo, he elaborated his ideas on the simple man in a series of retreat notes he jotted down in preparation for his eightieth birthday. He contrasted such a man with those wise in the ways of the world. The simple man was not ashamed to profess the Gospel, even in the face of opposition and ridicule, before all men and on all occasions. However he was treated, he never lost his peace of mind. Of course, though simple, he must "always be sustained by a wise and gracious prudence." But such "prudence" was to be understood in the Gospel sense. The simple and prudent man was one who

having chosen a good, and still more a great and noble objective, never loses sight of it, but overcomes all obstacles and carries it through to completion. On every issue he distinguishes between what is essential, and what is non-essential. The latter never diverts him: he concentrates all his energies on the essence. He looks to God alone. He trusts in God, and this is the basis of his efforts.

He added that the conjunction of simplicity and prudence could be put another way:

Simplicity is love: prudence is thought. Love prays: the intelligence keeps watch. "Watch and pray": the harmony is perfect. Love is like the cooing dove. The intelligence is like the snake which never stumbles because, before it advances, it first explores with its head the unevenness of the ground.

As John, to use his own image, explored the unevenness of the ground, his confidence in himself, and of others in him, became stronger. In his earliest speeches and public writings as pope, it is notable that he often justified his statements by reference to his predecessors, above all to Pius XII. These references, though never wholly abandoned, became fewer and more perfunctory as he proceeded. Perhaps to his surprise, certainly to his constant delight, he realized that his words were valued because they came from him, that he had established himself as a person who carried great authority, who was loved and obeyed *sua propria persona*. Within weeks of coming to the throne, he perceived that he was already accepted, not just as a notable head of the church, but as a world figure. As the horizon expanded, he grew to fill it. In Advent, 1959, after his first full year in office, he noted: "The experience of this first year gives me light and strength in my efforts to straighten, to reform, and tactfully and patiently to make improvements in everything."

"Improvements in everything" must be understood in the sense John wished to convey. He knew that his time was limited. He did not believe he could transform every aspect of the church, even were this desirable. There were things he felt he could not tackle. He was quite incapable of organizational reform. To him, the Curia was a mystery. He did not understand the mechanics, or sympathize with the spirit, of the bureaucratic machine, and therefore made no attempt to reform it, or even to remove those within it who were clearly opposed to his general policies. He has been criticized on this score; and it is true that, by leaving the Curia virtually intact he raised difficulties for himself. But then we must remind ourselves of the kind of man John was. He knew his own limitations. He judged, almost certainly wisely, that his comparative lack of administrative experience made him ill-fitted to undertake a structural reform which would have to be fundamental to be effective at all. He knew enough about bureaucracy to grasp that it was no use producing a blueprint for change: a plan for reform had to be followed up by detailed supervision and rigorous checks over a long period. It would be a full-time job for a pope in the prime of life. He had neither the time nor the energy for such a task. If he embarked on curial reform that, in effect, would constitute his pontificate; and he felt he had more important things to do — and things he knew he could do well, which his whole life had prepared him to do. Then again, tackling the Curia would mean not merely publicly opposing himself to the dominant faction there, but building up a faction of his own, identifying himself with a party. And John was not a party man, as he often liked to say. He wanted to be the pope of everyone. Granted the circumstances, and his own temperament, he thought he could operate more effectively through the existing institution than by trying to fashion a new one.

Hence, almost his first act was to raise Tardini to the cardinalate and confirm him officially in his post as secretary of state. When Tardini died, John replaced him by Cardinal Cicognani, who had had a highly successful spell as apostolic delegate in the United States, and was otherwise well qualified, but was generally ranked as a conservative. John's manner of making this key appointment was highly characteristic. He did not discuss Tardini's replacement until after the old cardinal had been buried. Late on the evening of the funeral (John often liked to do business in the evening) he summoned Cicognani and told him that, during the funeral, he had looked at the members of the Sacred College assembled round the coffin, and made his decision. Would he become secretary of state? Cicognani was taken aback, and demurred. He said he was too old for the job; that he was not very well; and that in any case he must have time to think. John turned to other subjects, and chatted away happily for half an hour. Then he said: "Now you have had time to think. Will you accept?" Cicognani did so, and served John loyally, though without any apparent enthusiasm.

John was also unadventurous in his general approach to the Sacred College. It is true he doubled its size. He held his first consistory on 15 December 1958, when he created twenty-three new cardinals; in all he added fifty-four members to the College, an unprecedented increase, especially in such a short pontificate. These included the first Indian cardinal, and the first African. But many of the new creations were curial officials, some very old men, given a red hat as a reward for long years of service. John was disturbed by the pluralistic tendencies in the Curia, and made discreet efforts to persuade certain cardinals, who held a multiplicity of offices, to resign all but one. He was also anxious that the more elderly cardinals should relinquish active appointments. But he did not choose to issue formal commands. John was a man of great generosity and delicacy, who hated the idea of hurting the feelings of anyone, especially a senior prelate who had devoted his life to serving the papacy. He made his wishes clear: that was all. Some responded. Cardinal Tisserant, still hale and vigorous, surrendered his principal posts. Others flatly declined, and Pope John was hurt. He was heard to say, on more than one occasion: "They have refused the Pope. They have refused the Pope." It was to him sad, and almost incredible, that those honored with the highest offices in the church should lack that simple spirit of pure obedience to the pontiff which he had made a salient principle of his career. But he did not insist; it was against his nature, and he was unwilling to expose himself to the charge that he was dealing harshly with men scarcely older than himself.

John also avoided any contact, so far as it was possible, with the financial business of the Vatican. In the mid-1950s, Pius XII had employed Jackson Martinelli to advise the Curia on modern financial and administrative controls. Martinelli had observed: "There is not much difference between Standard Oil of New Jersey and the Catholic Church's operations. The only difference is that Standard produces oil and the Catholic Church produces a way of thought and life." Pope John felt that such a difference, even if it could be categorized in such crude terms, was transcendental. Such a world was utterly alien to him; he did not understand it, and knew he was too old to learn. He thus perpetuated the financial structure which had emerged under Pope Pius. Was this cowardice? Perhaps so; but John had his soul to save; he did not consider he could embrace such a sphere without defilement; like any good Catholic he had learned always to "avoid the occasion of sin." His only interference in finance was true to character. In 1959, apparently without consulting anyone, he raised the salaries of Vatican employees by nearly fifty percent. The raise was entirely justified, indeed long overdue. The Vatican, like other conservative institutions, is slow to take note of the ravages of inflation. But John's abrupt decision caused confusion and some embarrassment. With the increase, the total Vatican payroll, as Tardini revealed, rose to about $7,250,000 a year. Neither the financial department of the Vatican City State, nor the Administration of the Patrimony of the Holy See, seemed able, or at any rate willing, to provide the extra money. In financial matters, the Vatican functions along pre-nineteenth century lines: that is, there is no central office of receipt and disbursement — no treasury control, as we would say — and different spending departments have their own sources of finance, or liens on other sources of revenue, as was the practice in most eighteenth-century states. John's decision thus placed an unexpected strain on a weird and delicate piece of antique machinery. Eventually, Tardini solved the problem by drawing on a special fund (not exactly secret service money, but something very like it) administered by the secretariat of state. John realized he had trodden on a hornets' nest, and thereafter he left finance strictly alone. Indeed, though not a man who normally shirked any topic of conversation, he disliked talking about the administrative and financial side of the Holy See, taking refuge in jokes. Asked how many people worked in the Vatican State, he replied:

"About half of them." Curiously enough, however, he himself was instrumental in raising the papal revenues. The enormous publicity he received, and the impact of his personality on people throughout the world, led to a substantial increase in voluntary and unsolicited contributions to papal funds.

But if John made no basic changes in the structure of the Vatican, he revolutionized its atmosphere. Much of the monarchical protocol of the court he simply dismantled. He refused to wear the tiara, except on one or two very formal occasions. Nor would he wear the traditional satin slippers, thereby imitating Leo X (1513–1521), though, unlike Leo, he did not go around in hunting boots, preferring tough black buckled shoes. He stopped Vatican officials bowing three times when they entered his room, leaving it backwards, or addressing him on their knees. He did not like to sit behind a desk when talking to visitors: he installed them, and himself, in comfortable armchairs. He made his third-floor study in the Vatican Palace bright with Bergamesque furniture and Venetian glass. There was a huge Murano chandelier, and a crib with painted glass figures (this replaced the fine set of carved Bavarian wood, which Pius XII had brought back from Germany, but which he displayed only on one day a year). His rooms were full of knickknacks presented to him by friends and visitors, and were painted in sunny colors (later restored to grim shades of gray by Pope Paul VI), but there was nothing of great value, except a few rare books he had acquired. Indeed, he was disturbed, even dismayed, by the immense quantity of treasures he found in the Vatican. What was to be done with them? They were not his to dispose of, but entailed possessions, heirlooms, of which he was a mere life tenant. So far as possible, he had them shifted to the Vatican Museum for public display; and he introduced a far more liberal policy of access, both to the museum and library, and the secret archives, and to the Vatican City State generally, especially the gardens, which had been fiercely guarded under his predecessor. The Vatican lost its air of somber privacy, and became a bustling place. Some things John did feel able to give away: on his accession he was shown a roomful of presents, many of great value — monstrances, chalices, embroidered vestments and so forth — given to Pius XII and simply stored. These, and other unregistered properties, he distributed throughout the world. But, like other popes before him, he was overawed by the patrimony of the Holy See. How could it be right for a church of poverty to possess such wealth? But how could he, a humble transient, disturb the arrangements of centuries, millennia almost?

Within the palace, he broke through the cocoon Pius had woven around himself. He roved up and down its corridors and staircases, poked his head into obscure offices, and rambled through the gardens and buildings of the park. John was inquisitive, and delighted in any discovery, especially of an antiquarian kind. A third-century statue of the antipope Hippolytus, long since buried in shame, was unearthed; John had it restored and installed in an honorable place at the entrance to the Vatican Library — it was a chance to exercise charity to a dead, and possibly maligned, ecclesiastic. He was also gregarious. He stopped and chatted to officials, secretaries, cleaners and gardeners, displaying his enormous repertoire of jokes, peasant proverbs, biblical and patristic sayings, snippets from the *obiter dicta* of saints and holy men. He soon became a familiar figure in the confines of the City State.

And not only in its confines. Pius XII, like all his predecessors from Pio Nono onwards, had rarely left the Vatican; his seclusion was part of his fortress mentality. When he did so, he had himself driven at great speed, with a motorcycle escort — he shared with Mother Pasqualina a passion for fast driving. John saw himself not only as pope, but as bishop of Rome, charged with pastoral duties to the city and its suburbs. He went into Rome constantly, and had himself driven slowly, so that he could see and be seen. Often he left the car and walked the streets, talking to people. At the outset of his papacy he caused a sensation by visiting Rome's Regina Coeli prison. As he told the convicts: "You cannot come to me, so I came to you." One of them, sentenced to life imprisonment for murder, asked if he would find forgiveness. John took him into his arms, and embraced him on both cheeks. On Christmas Day 1958 — his first as pope — he went to Rome's two children's hospitals, the Gesu Bambino and the Santo Spirito, and talked to the sick children at their bedsides. These occasions attracted immense publicity. They might have been regarded simply as exercises in successful public relations. In fact, John had the capacity to transform such occasions into real events. It was plain to anyone present — the photos and movie-film taken tell the same story — that his concern for the unfortunate, and the sick, was genuine and natural. It was part of his pastoral gift. John could make himself at ease with all conditions of men; and with children he had the magic touch. One small boy told him he had not yet decided whether to be a pope or a policeman. "I would go in for the police if I were you," said John. "Anyone can become Pope — look at me." If the style was homely, the tone of John's conversation self-deprecatory, there was no mistaking the dignity of the man, or the dignity of his office. John had a deep, resonant voice, and he pronounced his words slowly and distinctly, seeming to give them extra weight: he had the power of imparting freshness to a trivial and familiar phrase. He was impressive to look at, too: a big man in every sense, with a broad, sculptured head — almost bald now — elephantine ears, deep, lustrous eyes, a gaze that could be stern, though usually benign; and a smile that seemed to encompass the world. He was a father figure, and he looked it.

John was delighted with the success of his frequent excursions into Rome, and occasionally traveled further. He felt he was too old to get involved in state visits abroad — the idea of a jet-age pope had to await his successor — but in 1962, on the eve of the council, he went on pilgrimage to Assisi, the home of Saint Francis, and to Loreto, one of the most popular Marian shrines in Italy, which contains a house that medieval peasants supposed had been transported from Nazareth by angels. He used the state railway carriage built for Pio Nono but which no pope had ever entered; indeed, he was the first pope to leave Rome since Pio Nono's re-entry into the

Vatican. He read the newspaper accounts of his travels with great pleasure (he was always an avid reader of newspapers), though he found the adulatory tone in which he was described a little cloying. He tried to persuade the *Osservatore Romano,* in particular, to scrap the hieratic phraseology with which it referred to the supreme pontiff, but without success. At least, however, he stopped the practice of *Osservatore* reporters taking dictation from the pope on their knees — a ridiculous procedure which had grown up under Pius XII.

John held regular public and semipublic audiences, and made some excellent little speeches to them, though he paid far less attention to this aspect of his work than his predecessor. He liked to talk to people face to face; he enjoyed a dialogue. Moreover, he had to spend a large portion of his time making himself accessible to curial officials, senior Italian clergy, and above all visiting prelates from throughout the world. Here, Pius XII had been remiss: it was a major and bitter grievance against him. Except at breakfast, John never took his meals alone. Cardinals, bishops, monsignors, and often simple parish priests — as well as laymen — lunched and dined with him almost daily. These were not big parties, but good food was served, and first-class wine. The talk was general, and John abandoned the protocol that no topic could be broached until the pope first introduced it. Heads of state, senior clerics from other religious denominations, politicians and opinion-formers were also welcome, and came in increasing numbers. These private visits were very informal: chats round a coffee table. John was delighted to receive Mrs. Kennedy, and insisted on calling her Jackie. Sometimes John was advised that he ought to stick more closely to the manners and phraseology of a head of state, and he did his best to comply; but the effort usually broke down before the audience was five minutes old, and then the familiar jokes and the gossip would take over, to prepare the way for relaxed, serious conversation. Pope John was rather like Dr. Samuel Johnson's old friend at Pembroke College: "He tried hard to be a philosopher, but cheerfulness would keep breaking in." As John put it himself: "We must blow off the dust from the throne of Constantine which has been lying too long on the Chair of Peter." Before he had been in office a year, Palmiro Togliatti, the subtle and open-minded leader of the Italian Communist party, remarked: "The age of Constantine is dead." Pietro Nenni, leader of the Italian left-wing Socialists, summed up the new pope in a memorable phrase: "In place of the hieratical papal figure who intimidates there came the pastor who touches the heart." This tribute gave John much satisfaction: it indicated that he was succeeding in his aim.

Nor was his pastoral work merely symbolic. It was professional and thorough, detailed even. For the first time since the early eighteenth century, he held, as pope, a synod of the Rome diocese. The decision to hold the synod was one of the earliest taken in his pontificate, and the meeting, which took place in the week of January 24–31 1960, in the Cathedral of the City of Rome, Saint John Lateran, was preceded by a year of intense preparation. John's motives for holding the synod were various: it was the episcopal practice he had been taught by Bishop Radini, and which he had followed as patriarch of Venice; it was an opportunity to demonstrate, in anticipation of the Ecumenical Council, that pastoral clergy and professional theologians could be brought to work in teamship together, and produce concrete and comprehensive results during a limited period of time; and it provided him with a convenient platform from which to outline his ideas about the nature of pastoral work, the conduct and role of the parochial clergy, and the mission of the church in the world. It was not intended to adumbrate either the decisions of the council or its methods of work. The council was to be a free, legislative gathering of the world episcopate. The synod, by contrast, was a demonstration of how a bishop should regulate the clergy of his diocese and their work. In the twelve months before January 1960, senior priests of the diocese, assisted by theologians, drew up the texts of 755 synodal decrees, governing almost every aspect of Christian life in the modern world. During the synod, these documents were read, and discussion and amendments invited; the final decrees were promulgated six months later, at the end of June. During the synod, John himself provided a commentary on the proposed decrees, in a series of five talks he gave to the assembled clergy.

The work of the synod concentrated chiefly on the means whereby every member of the church, regular and secular priests, nuns, brothers and laymen and laywomen, could use the spiritual resources of their faith to bring the Christian message to the world. The decrees laid down what is, in effect, a detailed guide to the Christian way of life, and in particular the behavior of those in Holy Orders. In some respects, as has been mentioned

before, Pope John was a strict disciplinarian. He took
the highest possible view of the priestly office, and expected those who held it to conform to rigorous standards of conduct. To his mind, a priest was quite different
from ordinary people: and, as an external sign of this
division, he must look different and behave differently.
Thus the decrees reaffirmed the requirement that priests
of the Rome diocese wear the cassock in public, and have
the crown of the heads shaved (the tonsure). They were
forbidden to attend public performances of a profane
nature, from the opera to race meetings. John was quite
adamant on these points. Though gentle and charitable
on all occasions, and always slow to rebuke, he did not
hesitate to indicate his displeasure when he saw priests
behaving in a manner he felt to be unbecoming. Thus,
when he visited the English seminarists at their summer
villa in the Alban Hills, he was uncomfortable when
treated to a performance of a Gilbert and Sullivan oper-
etta. Gilbert and Sullivan has for many years been a
standby of the English College in Rome: the seminarists perform these harmless little musical plays with great
skill and enthusiasm. Naturally, as an Italian devotee of
"real" opera, John could not be expected to find this
English version much to his taste. But he was worried,
rather, by the idea of men training to be priests performing opera at all; and he said that, in his view, devotional
music would have been more appropriate. He displayed
the same severity in his attitude to TV: it was, he said,
a baneful influence, and he recommended priests not to
watch it.

On the other hand, the acts of the synod also reflect

John's spirit of charity. He had always been distressed by the systematic, and often ferocious, manner in which the clergy had been traditionally encouraged to boycott priests who had fallen into sin and disgrace. Article 35, which John wrote himself, specifically lays down: "Priests labouring under censure or other penalty, of who have perhaps unhappily left the church, should never cease to confide in the mercy of the Lord and the humaneness and decency of ecclesiastical superiors. Other priests, especially those who were joined to them in friendship, motivated by heavenly charity, should sedulously strive to cultivate this trust in their minds . . . no one is to be deprived of the friendliness of his fellow priests, or of consolation in his adversities, or even of temporal assistance should the circumstances call for it." This decree involved a revolution in the church's attitude, and marked an important stage in the dismantling of the fortress mentality. It reflected John's overwhelming belief that humanity is not divided into friends and enemies of the church but consists of winnable souls, whose relationship to the church varies in degree, but not in kind. Later, he wrote a letter of encouragement to a new order, set up in the United States, to look after priests who have broken their vows:

> These men are our brothers, pilgrims in life. In the dedication of their young lives they did not count the cost. If now they have been wounded in the fray, it is our duty to help them, for they are our brothers, our sick brothers. If the Good Shepherd will go after the sheep that is lost, how much more will he seek out the shepherd himself, should he stray in the mountain mists?

The image of the shepherd and the sheep was the dominant one of John's pontificate; he evoked it on endless occasions. Though his ministry was epitomized in the summoning of the council, and his two great encyclicals — which we will examine in the following chapters — it expressed itself just as naturally and completely in John's day-to-day conduct as a pastoralist and custodian of souls. He saw himself not so much as an intermediary between God and man, but as a natural and ordained conduit through which God's love for humanity flowed. On the one hand, God moved the pope to action; on the other, the pope radiated God's love. This was not the triumphalism of doctrine and temporal power: it was the universalism of Christian charity expressed through the papal office. Thus, John wrote in 1961:

> The various initiatives of a pastoral character which mark this first stage of my papal apostolate have all come to me as pure, tranquil, loving, I might even say silent, inspirations from the Lord, speaking to the heart of his poor servant, who, through no merit of his own save that very simple merit of mere acquiescence and obedience, without discussion, has been able to contribute to the honour of Jesus and the edification of souls.

And again, in the same year, commenting on the text "Feed my sheep":

> There is great authority in these words: the investiture of the Pope with his task as universal shepherd, in answer to his thrice repeated assurance of love, an assurance he gives to Jesus, who has deigned to ask for it with gentle insistence. It is love, then, that matters . . . the law of love

which sustains, inspires and adorns everything . . . the foundation of Holy Church, a foundation which is simultaneously visible and invisible, Jesus being invisible to the eyes of our flesh, and the Pope, the Vicar of Christ, being visible to the whole world.

John, in short, took the most elevated view of the pope's role in the divine dispensation for man. It was, quite simply, the most important office in the world. But it was an office based not on power but on affection. The remarkable achievement of his personality was that he was able to persuade multitudes of people, including many millions of non-Catholics, to accept this definition of his office — largely because they accepted his own capacity to fill it. John was aware of his success. He took no credit for it. The response to his pontificate merely, he wrote, "confirms the wisdom of the principle of waiting on God, and expressing with faith, modesty and confident enthusiasm the good inspiration of the grace of Jesus, who rules the world and guides it . . ." He often repeated the text: "The Lord is our lawgiver: he will carry and save us." Or, as he put it on another occasion: "The Lord holds in His all-powerful hands the threads of human history and directs it towards His own ends of goodness and grace."

What were those ends, in the particular context of John's pontificate? He had spoken, just after his election, of opening the windows of the church to receive, and be received by, the world. Under his leadership, this process took concrete and deliberate form in three monumental acts of policy, which we will now look at in turn.

EIGHT

The Radical Shepherd

OF THE THREE MAJOR ACTS of John's pontificate, the Ecumenical Council was promulgated in January 1959 and held its opening session in the autumn of 1962; the "social encyclical," *Mater et Magistra,* was published in May 1961; and the "international encyclical," *Pacem in Terris,* followed in April 1963. These three acts were very much interconnected; they were decisive expressions of a general policy which had a unity springing from John's concept of the church and its role in the world. But for purposes of clarity it is more convenient to analyze the two encyclicals together in this chapter, and recount the origins and progress of the council in the following.

John's overall object of policy was an ambitious one: to bring the Roman Catholic church back into the position he regarded as its natural right, at the center of world affairs. He considered that it had been deprived of this position by the isolationist, or "besieged fortress" policy of Pius IX and his successors. He did not believe that this radical change could be wholly accomplished during the few remaining years of his life. But he intended to make a start, and create a momentum which would continue to carry the church forward after his death. The new policy was to be accomplished in three ways. First, the Catholic church would reestablish itself in the center of worldwide Christian action, and thus enhance the influence of Christianity as such, by extending the hand of friendship to Christians of other denominations. Secondly, papal diplomacy would exert itself to create bridges between East and West, and between the advanced and the developing peoples, thus making its contribution to ending the Cold War and reducing the barriers between rich and poor nations. Thirdly, in order to accomplish these two objects, the Catholic church itself must experience an *aggiornamento* — a modernization and adjustment to the world.

Though Pope John was always absolutely clear in his own mind about his general aim, he was supremely pragmatic in its execution, and he adjusted both the chronology and the form of his acts of state in accordance with the changing situation, and the response which his pontificate was evoking within and outside the church. During the first two years of his pontificate he was building up a team of close personal advisers and agents. These included Cardinal Bea, whom he had inherited from Pius XII, and whom he entrusted with the organization of the new Secretariat for Christian Unity, which was to play a key role in the preparation of the council and its first session; Mgr. Pietro Pavan, lecturer in social economics at the Lateran University; Mgr. Agostino Ferrari Toniolo, Professor of Comparative Labor Law at the Lateran; Mgr. Sante Quadri, a senior official of the Catholic Workers' Organization (ACLI); and Mgr. Luigi Civardi, one of the leaders of Catholic Action, who also acted as his personal confessor. The last four were responsible for much of the drafting of *Mater et Magistra,* and the enthusiastic reception accorded to this encyclical led John to keep the team in being as a sort of private inner cabinet. All four (as well as Bea) were given important duties on the Council Preparatory Commissions; and, in addition, they were instructed by John to prepare the text of a second major encyclical, variously described as "fundamental" and "revolutionary," dealing with the church's views on international order. This, of course, was *Pacem in Terris.* It was, in fact, in draft form during the summer of 1962, and John's original intention was to publish it on the eve of the council's first session. But John had a keen, if instinctive, nose for publicity, and set great store by the exact timing of his public pronouncements. Thus he kept in reserve a number of policy statements ready for publication should the occasion arise. In the case of *Pacem in Terris,* he decided in September 1962 that it must not be allowed to conflict with the opening of the council, which was clearly going to receive enormous coverage in the world's press. If the two events coincided, either the impact of the council would be muted, or the significance of the encyclical would be lost while attention was focused on the council. So he delayed publication until after the first session, and the encyclical was launched the following spring. This change of plan was undoubtedly justified by events.

Although *Mater et Magistra* deals mainly with social problems, and *Pacem in Terris* with international ones, they ought to be considered together because there is considerable overlap, and the second is to some extent a development from the first. Collectively, too, they illuminate both the methodology and the tone of John's teaching. E. E. Y. Hales, whose analysis of the encyclicals is the most thorough and convincing so far published, draws attention to what he terms "a new note of hesitancy" in the Johannine teaching. Of course an encyclical is a personal expression of the pope's opinion, a pastoral message, as it were, to a worldwide congregation. Though it carries great weight, it does not necessarily have, for Catholics, the authority of absolute law. Nevertheless, in the past, papal encyclicals have undoubtedly assumed the voice of a command, and as they were often published in response to a particular situation, and to problems which have since changed their nature, or disappeared, the papacy has an embarrassing legacy of *obiter dicta*, expressed in the most categorical terms, which are now palpably invalid, or even nonsense. In his teaching, John did not hesitate, if only by inference, to repudiate the views of predecessors. He abandoned completely the old dogmatic device of distinguishing between *thesis* and *hypothesis* — that is, the unequivocal statement that a certain concept (such as democracy) is intrinsically bad, qualified by the hypothesis that it should be tolerated where it has been accepted, and the church is unavoidably obliged to operate a *modus vivendi*. John regarded this distinction as evasive if not downright dishonest: popes had a duty to make up their minds. When necessary, he simply contradicted previous popes. Thus, he rejected *in toto* such reactionary political encyclicals as Gregory XVI's *Mirari Vos* and *Singulari Nos,* and the *Quanta Cura* of Pius XI, to which was attached, as appendix, the Syllabus of Errors of Pius IX. If we take *Mater et Magistra* and *Pacem in Terris* together, they effectively demolish most of the internationalist, social, economic and political teachings of the popes for the previous hundred years, with the one exception of Leo XIII's *Rerum Novarum* (and other papal documents deriving from it), which Pope John explicitly praised and classified as inspirational. But if John was ruthless in dismissing the views of his predecessors, he was diffident in putting forward his own. He is quite clear in his own mind what he thinks, at any rate on most subjects, and he set his opinions down plainly. But he is anxious to point out that these are essentially his own personal thoughts; popes have been wrong before, and he also may be shown to be mistaken, or more likely outdated, by future events. These are pastoral interpretations of the truth, made in a certain context, and at a given moment of time; nothing more. It was one of John's central beliefs that the church, while possessing the essence of truth for all time, must be constantly employed in reinterpreting it in the light of changing needs. That, indeed, was the object of his council; and that was the methodology of his encyclicals. If he had been a less diffident man, he might have added that it was also the message of Paul and the other Apostles in their epistles, which were to be read and understood in a similar spirit.

The Johannine encyclicals have a further characteristic, which springs from their author's own temperament. They are optimistic. They radiate confidence. To be sure, the world is a place where evil sometimes flourishes, where the good go unrewarded, and the wicked unpunished. But it is also, in God's providence, a place of opportunities and experiments, some intrinsically good, others to be turned to good account. Pius XII and his predecessors, it seemed to John, had largely contented themselves with registering protests against the evils of the world; but the church also had a duty to recognize the opportunities, and teach Christians — and others — how to take advantage of them. For his part, that was what he intended to do.

In setting down his social teaching in *Mater et Magistra,* John did his best to emphasize its continuity with previous teaching. He was not anxious to repudiate earlier popes more than was absolutely necessary. This led him into some well-meaning exaggerations, what might almost be termed a falsification of the record. Just as Pius XI had issued his social document, *Quadragesimo Anno,* on the fortieth anniversary of *Rerum Novarum,* so John published *Mater et Magistra* on its seventieth. He refers to Leo's encyclical as "the Magna Carta of Catholic social teaching," and writes of "Our responsibility to take up this torch which our great predecessors lighted . . . a torch to lighten the pathways of all who would seek appropriate solutions." Of course it may be that John tended to see Leo's teaching against the back-

ground of his own youth, when it had certainly appeared
innovatory. But in actual fact, what John taught has
really very little in common with any previous papal
pronouncement. Both Leo and Pius XI had rejected
socialism in any form, though the latter conceded that
there were degrees of evil. Both rejected trades unionism,
as we understand it, and though they accorded the workers certain elementary rights, they conceived that such
rights should be granted from above, rather than seized
from below. Both regarded democracy as an evil in itself,
and Christian monarchy as an ideal form of government.
Leo wanted the workers organized in a medieval system
of guilds, or a vertical trades union structure including
employers, of a type imposed by General Franco in fascist
Spain. Both rejected the materialism of unrestricted capitalism, but they accepted the capitalist system as such, as
being a modern form of private property, which they
related to the family as an indispensable element in the
social background of Christianity. Where Pius XI criticized capitalism he was concerned with spiritual, rather
than social, evils. Thus, he wanted to regulate the hours
of work imposed by employers to enable workmen to
perform their religious duties, on Sunday and holy days
of obligation. Equally, he objected to fascist centralism,
and advocated the devolution of power, because he feared
that an authoritarian, highly centralized secular state
might be a threat to the church. But he was not opposed
to authority as such, provided it was exercised in accordance with the church's teaching.

When, therefore, John writes in *Mater et Magistra* that
he merely intends to "confirm and make more specific"

the words of his predecessors, this is more a courteous genuflection than a statement of fact. John dismissed any notion of a medieval guild-type organization for labor, or any system for improving working-class standards which is imposed by authority. The workers have a right to organize themselves to secure their legitimate desires, indeed a duty to do so. What is more, the population as a whole has a perfect right to use the state to supply defects in a system based on private enterprise. Here was an important departure: John was, in effect, endorsing the concept of a welfare state, not as something which was permissible only, but as a desirable good in itself. Pius XII, for instance, had been worried by what he saw as unwholesome implications in such welfare devices as communal kitchens, free health services, and universal free education. He thought them potentially, if not actually, socialist in inspiration and purpose. They tended to degrade the individual, destroy the special role of wives and mothers, and undermine family life. John, on the other hand, thought the state had a right, and often a duty, to see to it that all had the necessities of life, among which he included education and medical services. Private charity, on which Pius XII relied, was desirable and commendable; but the state must step in when charity was not enough. This new role of the state was, from a Christian viewpoint, intrinsically welcome because it was "an increase in social relationships" and a "development in the social life of man." "It is an effect and a cause," he wrote, "of the growing intervention of the state even in matters of such intimate concern to the individual as health and education, the choice of a career, and the care

and rehabilitation of the physically and mentally handi-
capped."

Where John's predecessors had deplored the encroach-
ments of the state as an interference with human freedom,
he stood the argument on its head. Indeed, he advanced
the central socialist argument, put forward by his contemporaries like Aneurin Bevan in Britain, and Pietro
Nenni in Italy, that the assumption of responsibilities by
the state is an extension of freedom. State intervention,
he wrote, "makes it possible for the individual to exercise
many of his personal rights . . . such as the right to . . .
preserve himself in good health, to receive further education and a more thorough professional training; the
right to housing, work, suitable leisure and recreation."
What John was doing was to revolutionize the definition
of basic individual rights which the church had hitherto
upheld. These had been confined to mere subsistence;
John now acknowledged that every individual had the
right to a decent life — and he added that it was the
responsibility of the state to see that this right was
guaranteed.

John recognized that the enlargement of the rights and
duties of the state might give rise to dangers. Thus: "a
multiplicity of restrictive laws and regulations in every
department of human life . . . narrows the sphere of a
person's freedom of action . . . [and conspires] to make it
difficult for a person to think independently of outside
influences, to act on his own initiative, to exercise responsibility and express and fulfill his own personality." But
this possible threat did not, in itself, constitute a reason
for opposing the welfare state. Instead, safeguards should

be provided. Where the state interfered it should do so, if possible, through agencies which had a real degree of independence of government, and operated under their individual charters. What he had in mind was probably the state corporations, set up in Britain during the post-war Labour government, to administer the public sector of industry: mining, the railways, gas and electricity, the central bank, and so forth. John believed in the distribution of power, and the creation of countervailing forces to balance the enlargement of central government. And he thought the process of public enlightenment would help to act as a guarantee against an all-powerful state molding the thinking of individuals. The media, in which he included "the press, cinema, radio and TV," had a positive role to play: they must, of course, operate "within the framework of a moral order," but, by spreading the truth, and offering a variety of opinions, they could keep the monolithic state in check. Mass education was even more important. Where Pius XII had been prepared to go no further than advocate "higher education for children of the working-class who are exceptionally intelligent and well-disposed" — the latter qualification implying some form of political and religious control of entry to technical colleges and universities — John wanted "provision for all the citizens to share as far as they are able in their country's cultural advantages."

Of course, John could offer no absolute proof that the enlargement of the state's duties would not, in some respects, diminish the individual. This was one reason why he wanted to see a much wider diffusion of property. The man without property, the mere wage slave, was much more likely to fall victim to an omnipotent state than one who could stand on his own ground. Hence a revitalized yeoman-peasant community was essential to the health of the state. Here he thought primarily in Italian terms, though much of what he said applied to France, Spain, the Balkans and the Near East, India, Africa and parts of Latin America — the semideveloped and the under-developed world generally. John knew from his own experience why peasant farmers were leaving the land: cultivating a small farm could rarely provide the lux-uries which men increasingly regarded as necessities. On the other hand, again from his own experience, he re-garded a satisfied peasant community, revolving round the family farm, as an excellent framework for the Chris-tian life, and indeed for much else — political stability, for example. In *Mater et Magistra* he wrote at consider-able length on agricultural problems, expressing his own long-held views, and descending to a degree of detail more characteristic of Pius XII, and which he himself normally avoided. The life of a peasant farmer, he noted, was not an easy one; it might bring less in terms of mate-rial rewards than work in industry, or emigration. On the other hand, growing food had "a dignity all its own." The family farm was the most socially desirable unit of production. Farmers must form cooperatives for the pro-vision of machinery and fertilizers, and unions "to ac-quire a voice in political circles and in public adminis-tration. The lone voice is not likely to command much of a hearing in times such as ours." The state had a duty to help small farmers by improving road and rail com-munications, providing a water supply, building modern houses, and by providing health centers, schools and recreational facilities in country districts, where they were notoriously meager. Agriculture must be modernized by extensive state investment. Anything which narrowed the differential between farm incomes and industrial wages — lower taxes for farmers, state credit banks, provision of part-time or seasonal industrial work in farming districts — was to be encouraged.

John applied the same principles, though in considerably less detail, to the welfare of industrial workers. Small factories and business should be helped by taxation policy and cooperatives. Where possible workers should have a share in profits. Training and retraining schemes should be set up by the state. Workers should not be dismissed as mere "cogs in the machine." They had a right to a say in their economic destinies. The government should actively encourage these proposals, and should consult with unions as well as management before determining economic policy.

Having advocated a much wider role for government in society, John felt constrained to give some guidance on what form government should take. He said nothing about the concept of a Christian monarchy, hitherto the standby of papal political teaching. Presumably he thought that monarchy was, for all practical purposes, a dead issue. Some popes had condemned any popular form of elective government as intrinsically evil. Leo XIII had merely said that it was "not forbidden to give preference to moderate forms of popular government." In his Christmas message of 1944 Pius XII had reminded his listeners of this statement, and added that democratic parliaments

could not meet with ecclesiastical approval unless they
were comprised of "a select body of men of firm Christian
convictions" — needless to say, an impossible condition
to meet. John alludes to the system of government in both
his great encyclicals. He notes, and welcomes, that ordinary men and women are becoming increasingly aware
"of their personal dignity," and were expressing it by
becoming active in political life. Indeed: "A natural consequence of men's dignity is unquestionably their right
to take an active part in public life." This was not only
right in itself but an important guarantee against private injustice and the overwhelming power of the state.
As for the state itself, John declined to define its ideal
nature, or, as he put it, "a general ruling on the most suitable form of government . . . a major consideration will
be the prevailing circumstances and the condition of the
people." The function of the state was "to recognise, respect, coordinate, safeguard and promote the rights and
duties of the citizens." Hence its powers should be subject to definite limits. It existed to protect human rights,
not to create them, for rights are not man-given but God-
given, transmitted directly to the human individual by
the natural law. Hence it was vital that "a clear and precisely worded charter of principal human rights be formulated and incorporated into the constitutions of
states." There should be, in addition, a separation of
powers, at any rate between the judiciary and the executive, and John seems to have believed, likewise, that the
executive and the legislature should also be separate. Possibly he regarded the United States constitution, with its
embodiment of states' rights, its republican form, its uni-

versal vote, its separation of powers, and its written constitution enshrining basic human rights, as the best possible model, at least in theory. This certainly seems to be
the message of his teaching, and he indicates that democracy is the best system; but its application must "depend
upon the stage of development."

In any case, as John points out, constitutions are pieces
of paper; all depends on the spirit in which they are
worked. In the long run, the individual had to rely on
freedoms which went beyond the political, and institutions which were independent of the state. Of the latter,
the most important was the family, "the natural, primary
cell of human society." If the dignity of the individual
were ensured, and this involved the whole of his social
teaching, the family would naturally grow in strength.
Of course, within the family the individual had rights.
John did not share the view of Pius XII that women
should be placed in a different category, to be cosseted,
protected, revered and (in effect) condescended to by men.
He said nothing about Pius's voluminous teaching on the
special status of women, and the inference is that he regarded it as out of date and unhelpful. He noted, without
comment, that there was a rising demand for greater
rights for women. But he was unwilling to enter what he
clearly regarded as dangerous territory.

Where he was absolutely adamant was in his insistence
on total liberty of conscience. Here he demolished orthodox and traditional Catholic teaching. *Pacem in Terris*
states flatly that every human being has the right "to worship God in accordance with the right dictates of his own
conscience, and to profess his religion both in private

and in public." This embodied, therefore, one of President Roosevelt's four freedoms: the freedom of worship, something the Catholic church had never before acknowledged, indeed had specifically repudiated. It is true that John defends his view by saying that freedom of conscience had always been the teaching of the church. But the authorities he cites in fact deal only with the freedom of Christians, and in particular of Roman Catholics. The classic statement of the church's views had been put in the most honest and unvarnished terms in 1885, when Louis Veuillot, editor of the Catholic paper *L'Univers,* had told a gathering of French liberal and Protestant deputies: "When you are the masters, we claim perfect liberty for ourselves, as your principles require it. When we are the masters, we refuse it to you, as it is contrary to our principles." In recent decades, this insistence on a double standard had been somewhat glossed over by Catholic apologists, but it remained a practical fact that the Catholic church, while demanding religious freedom for itself everywhere, denied it to others when it was in a position to do so. John's ruling effectively ended this double standard. He did not merely tolerate, of necessity, the religious rights of others, whether non-Catholic Christians, Jews, Muslims or other sects; he accepted and recognized them, fully and completely. Now this was a very important departure, which had a bearing on a much wider sphere than the freedom of worship and the liberty of conscience, fundamental though these were. In a sense, John's initiative helped to emphasize the distinction between the fortress mentality of his predecessors, and his own outward-looking optimism. It meant that he no longer treated Catholics, and the rest of the human race, as two separate categories, the rights of the one being superior to the rights of the other. And this, in turn, established his credibility with the non-Catholic world. Pius XII's sincerity as an international moralist was fatally undermined by his evident belief that the rights of Catholics were the only ones worth upholding, or fighting for. John's universalism was accepted as genuine because he clearly believed, and stated, that liberty was indivisible. This statement was thus perhaps the most crucial in his career. It did more than any other to establish his *bona fides* and so his title to exercise leadership on the world stage.

As an advocate of freedom of worship, and liberty of conscience, Pope John would have been guilty, in an earlier age, of the heresy of "indifferentism." In his more general views of international affairs, he would certainly have been condemned, by Pius XII, as an unconscious ally, if not an active agent, of the Communist conspirarcy against the Catholic church. Pius had assumed that all men were, directly or indirectly, committed to the cause of Catholicism or against it. But John did not divide mankind into sheep and goats. All were souls to be saved. No individual was committed, by birth, upbringing, race, color, creed or nationality to a permanent posture. The pope was a universal father, whether or not he was acknowledged as such. He spoke for, and to, all men and women. It was an audacious claim, but one made in all humility. He appealed — he said it repeatedly — "to all men of good will." Although his right to speak universally derived from his position as leader of the Roman

Catholic community, it is remarkable that his references to his church and its claims — still less its uniqueness — are few and far between. His main encyclicals, indeed, deal only briefly, and by inference, with church matters. They are addressed to a wider audience. Moreover, such concern with the Catholic world as he did express tended to diminish as his pontificate progressed and he became conscious of his universalist mission. When he published *Mater et Magistra,* for instance, he was still preoccupied by the problems of Italian agriculture. By the time he wrote *Pacem in Terris,* such local considerations had fallen completely into the background of his thoughts. He had turned his back on Italian politics, which had obsessed the papacy since the revolution of 1848 and had tended to make its view of world affairs a mere reflection of the Italian situation. In *Pacem in Terris,* Pope John speaks as a father of all men, irrespective of their race, creed or continent. He regards himself as able to do this, he says, both as "Christ's vicar on earth," and as "the interpreter of the most ardent wishes of the whole human family, in the fatherly love we bear all mankind." Thus qualified, he felt he had a duty "to beg and beseech men, and particularly statesmen, to be unsparing of their labours and efforts to ensure that human affairs follow a rational and dignified course."

Other popes had asked for world peace; but it had been a peace qualified by conditions of their own making, shaped by a partisan analysis of the international situation, and arising from an exclusive view of their church's claims. John appealed for peace without qualification, without preconditions, and without *arrière-pensées.* He

was the first pope to acknowledge the context of a thermonuclear world. He recognized that this world was divided
by rival ideologies, and that his church had to express its
attitude towards them. But he doubted whether such
ideologies went sufficiently deep to justify absolute condemnation. In *Mater et Magistra* he had already admitted
the practical virtues of socialism, insofar as they embodied
benevolent state action. In *Pacem in Terris* he went
further, and indicated how a *modus vivendi* with communism could be reached. He distinguished between
communism as such, which he termed "a false philosophy," and many of its aspects, which might be welcome
in practical political programs, "even when such a pro-
gramme draws its origins and inspiration from such a
philosophy." He took the view that pragmatic consequences were more important than logical rigor, since
ideological theories were subject to practical considerations, as he put it. The *practice* of Communist states
might well contain "good and commendable elements."
Even if Communist leaders were committed, in theory,
to universal world revolution, it was possible, even likely,
that they would settle for peaceful coexistence when it
came to the point. This probability should be recognized,
and turned to good advantage. Therefore the world
should proceed, step by step, to work for a ban on the
testing of nuclear weapons, then a ban on nuclear warfare, then systematic disarmament. He appealed for negotiations, to be followed by treaties. There were, he
admitted — he was thinking of Pius XII's analysis of the
world — certain elements of injustice in international
arrangements. But he did not mention Eastern Europe,

or "the church of silence." In any case, the restoration of justice and liberty, while not forgotten, could wait. Granted the existence of nuclear weapons, "it is contrary to reason to maintain that war is a fit instrument with which to repair the violation of injustice." "Rollback" was a lost cause, an unrealizable objective. Mankind must take the world as it is, and attempt to effect improvements within a context which rules out war as a conceivable means of policy.

There were various means by which these "improvements" could be brought about. John devoted four paragraphs in *Pacem in Terris* to commending the world of the United Nations. He rejected the view of Pius XII that the secular character and origins of the U. N. Security Council was an obstacle to its acceptance; on the contrary, it was "a step towards the establishment of a juridical and political organisation of the world community." He made it clear that he was more concerned with the Third World of the undeveloped, uncommitted nations, than with the lost territories in Eastern Europe. As long ago as 28 November 1959, when he published his encyclical on missions, *Princeps Pastorum,* John had explicitly condemned colonialism and expressed his anxiety for the welfare of the undeveloped countries. In *Mater et Magistra* he had reiterated and expanded these views. Now, in *Pacem in Terris,* he reminded the world of his previous appeals "to the more wealthy nations to render every kind of assistance to those states which are still in the process of economic development," and added: "it is no small consolation to us to be able to testify here to the wide acceptance of our appeal . . ." But, he now laid down, these poorer nations must be helped "in a way which guarantees to them the preservation of their own freedom." He rejected not only colonialism but neo-colonialism, any attempt to attach political strings to economic aid. Power blocks or military alliances, even regional economic arrangements, were illegitimate unless they were entered into freely by all the participants. This was aimed both at the Warsaw Treaty and such regional pacts as the Baghdad Pact and SEATO.

Pope John's reasons for advancing this line of argument led him to a fundamental definition of the rights of nations. Previous popes had held no brief for national sovereignty. Indeed, with the example chiefly of the Catholic multinational empire of Austria in mind, they had openly defended the concept of empire, at any rate in certain circumstances. On various occasions, they had condemned attempts by Poles and Czechs, by the Belgians or the Irish, even by the Italians, to rise against their "legitimate" political authorities. Such actions, justifying violence and defiance of the law by virtue of the mythical rights of national statehood, were sinful. John brushed aside such reasoning. The collective right of a nation to national independence, he argued, is merely an extension of the rights of an individual, which it was the duty of the church to uphold. In Africa and Asia, he said, the church should not merely cease to oppose the winds of change, but should identify itself with them. The attempt to impose the allegedly superior modes of the Western way of life on peoples of diverse race and culture was wrong in itself and politically mistaken. He thought that the undeveloped countries "have often preserved in their ancient traditions an acute and vital awareness of the more important human values. To attempt to undermine this national integrity is essentially immoral. It must be respected, and as far as possible strengthened and developed, so that it may remain what it is: a foundation of true civilisation.

It followed from this recognition of the cultural, as well as the political, rights of poorer nations, that no distinctions could be made on the grounds of race and color. The Catholic church had never operated a color bar in theory; but John was bitterly aware that it had often given its countenance to regimes which operated one in practice. He was anxious that the church's condemnation of racialism should be stated with unequivocal clarity and great vehemence. Hence: "Truth calls for the elimination of every trace of racial discrimination, and the consequent recognition of the inviolable principle that all states are by nature equal in dignity." Men might differ widely in knowledge and wealth, but that was no reason why the more powerful should dominate the weaker, either in an individual or in a collective context. "The fact is that no one can be by nature superior to his fellows, since all men are equally noble in natural dignity." If this was true of men, it was also true of states, since "Each state is like a body, the members of which are human beings."

Pope John's acceptance of the liberal economic and political philosophy is so complete, and so consistent, and in such striking contrast with the attitudes of his predecessors, that it is important to point out those instances where he felt compelled to reject the thinking of his progressive contemporaries. The truth is, it was not so much intellectual as spiritual convictions which made him a radical. His philosophy of love, of gentleness and charity, which pervaded his whole view of the Christian life, compelled him always to act the part of the conciliator and reconciler, between fellow Christians, between Christians and non-Christians, between East and West, between rich and poor nations, between socialist and non-socialist. He refused to acknowledge that any dispute was inevitable and permanent; he invariably sought the common ground, in the confident belief that a common ground existed. This attitude, in the context of traditional papal intransigeance, made him appear a revolutionary. But in many respects he was a very old-fashioned gentleman. He believed in obedience, order, self-discipline and sobriety. He was easily shocked by improper language, impurity, unseemly dress or behavior. Where John was, laughter and good spirits were never far away. He sought at his court to generate an atmosphere of simple friendliness, and undoubtedly succeeded. But it was an atmosphere bounded by a strict observance of the Ten Commandments. The style of life he wished to re-create was the one he had known and admired in the house of Bishop Radini, half a century before. And this, of course, had been regulated by the faithful and unquestioning acceptance of canon law. It was not out of character that John appointed the conservative (though genial) Cardinal Ottaviani as secretary to the Holy Office, though he may have come to regret his choice. His attitude towards the much criticized Index of Prohibited Books was unadventurous. He thought that young priests,

in particular, should be discouraged from reading certain
works except under careful supervision. In a speech in
November 1959, he told members of a Congress of Ecclesiastical Censors that they should accept no compromise
which might be prejudicial "to the sacred deposit of the
doctrine or to the souls of the faithful." Of course, as we
shall see, John was anxious to encourage a free spirit of
inquiry in biblical, theological and moral studies. He
loathed persecution in any form, and would not permit
the hounding of those earnestly seeking the truth,
whether or not he agreed with their methods and conclusions. His own "natural inclination," as he put it, was
to "expound doctrine with calm and simplicity rather
than to underline strongly points of disagreement or the
negative aspects of thought and actions" (15 February
1959). But, while he was radical in his ecclesiastical, political and international diplomacy, his approach to doctrine
tended to be conservationist. His devotional life, as we
know from his diary, was traditional in flavor. Many
thought it odd that he prepared for his revolutionary
council by a pilgrimage to Assisi and Loreto, places (particularly the latter), sometimes associated with what
might be called the "mumbo jumbo" side of Italian
Catholicism. But John loved places associated with sanctity; he drew nourishment from them. He was strongly
opposed to official endorsement of superstition. Shortly
after his election, he brusquely denied a tale circulating
in Rome that he had seen a vision of Pius X. He allowed
the publication in the *Osservatore* of an article which
dealt severely with the supernatural experiences of previous popes, including Pius XII. But he always delighted

in devotional exercises springing from the lives of authenticated saints. This was an aspect of Catholicism he had no wish to change, not least because he found it so valuable in his own life.

Nor was he anxious to rush into liturgical changes, as many urged him to do. He favored cautious experiments, and he encouraged historical work on the origins of church ceremonial. But he was most reluctant to administer shocks to ordinary churchgoing Catholics, and it is difficult to believe that he would have welcomed the immense liturgical changes which have taken place since his death. He favored ecumenical services at appropriate times, and he had no prejudice against the use of the vernacular; on the contrary — in Istanbul he had pioneered both innovations. But he thought that Latin should remain the standard language of Latin Christianity. His patristic and historical studies had given him a good command of Latin, which he delighted to read. Indeed, he was always proud of his Latin, such as it was, and took great pains to speak it well in public. During his retreat before the opening of the council, a Latin expert, Father Ciappi, came to him every morning for a conversational exercise in Latin. He admired the language as a vehicle for the precise expression of complex thought: it was, he considered, a great enemy of ambiguity. It was also, in his view, an instrument of internationalism, to be jealously protected, especially in the context of his global diplomacy. Thus, on 22 February 1962, he published an Apostolic Constitution on Latin, *Veterum Sapientia,* which made the point: "The language of Rome, used in the church of the Latin rite, particularly between her priests from different territories, can once again give noble service to the work of pacification and unification." He did not accept the view that to support the use of Latin was to align oneself with the anti-progressive camp, though that, in effect, was what it did. His constitution, in fact, is a vehement defense of the language. It states that Latin is an aid to "highly intelligent thought and speech." So bishops and religious superiors were to be on their guard lest anyone under their jurisdiction "write against the use of Latin in the teaching of the higher sacred studies or in the liturgy." Professors and lecturers in clerical universities and seminaries who were unable to teach in Latin should be replaced. A new Latin Academy was to be set up to invent Latin words to describe modern phenomena. The Sacred Congregation of Seminaries was to draw up a standard syllabus for the teaching of Latin. Students for the priesthood were to study not only Latin but Greek. The publication of this constitution was timed to emphasize the fact that Latin was to be the language of the council. John ruled out simultaneous translation on the grounds that inaccurate translation would generate confusion. The use of Latin by the council, as will appear, proved a disadvantage. John was probably unaware of the extent to which even the ablest and most energetic prelates in the Anglo-Saxon speaking countries (to say nothing of the underdeveloped world) were simply unable to speak it. In the context of the council it did not serve, as John hoped, as an aid to international understanding but as a barrier to it. He might, therefore, have altered his ruling if he had lived to see the second session. But he would have taken the decision with great reluctance and misgivings: he considered Latin to be one of the most precious jewels of his church, to be treasured as an irreplaceable heirloom.

If John found comfort in many aspects of tradition, he was also very much a man of his times. He was sensitive and responded to the general preoccupations of his day. This helps to explain his enormous appeal to men and women of all races. He did not speak to them, as his predecessors had done, from a different age, but from their own. But this closeness to the problems of the day had its disadvantages. John's gospel of love was timeless; so was his instinct to conciliate. But his view of the world was very much of his period, and already it begins to have a faintly dated air. John was fully aware of this risk, and joyfully accepted the possibility that his words would soon be forgotten. It was enough if they served a useful purpose when they were uttered. He wanted to replace Cold Wars in all their forms, to substitute a healthy optimism for the hostility, suspicion, almost despair which he found at his accession. This was surely right in the period of his pontificate; today, however, John's optimism sometimes strikes a false note. Thus, he perhaps underrated the difficulties the world would experience in bridging the gap between the advanced and the backward nations. He thought that all nations should seek to create an industrial sector (without prejudice to agriculture), and that this could be brought about granted good will and ample supplies of aid. He had a confidence in the forces of internationalism, and in the ability of international agencies to harness them, which we would now regard as oversanguine. In *Pacem in Terris* he rejected the absolute sovereignty of nations. He argued that "economic, social, political and cultural problems which affect the universal common good . . . must be considered too difficult for the rulers of individual states to solve with any degree of success" — hence the need for a "universal authority." The world was organic — like the state, and the family. Thus, while states had equal rights, like people, they were also, like people, interdependent, and shared common duties to each other. Their relationships would be strengthened by the growth in authority and experience — and scope — of international bodies. John was a strong supporter of Unesco, with which he had had many contacts when nuncio in Paris, and he greatly admired the technical work of the Food and Agricultural Organization. He was convinced of the ability of the United Nations to grow into a genuine arbiter of international disputes.

John also took an optimistic view of the problems of world population and resources. In his day, the "population explosion" had not become a fashionable cause for concern. Some scientists, it is true, were already issuing warnings, but the magnitude and intractability of the threat were not yet generally understood. Still less was there then any widespread anxiety about the exhaustion of natural resources. Hence, John was not confronted with a universal demand, inside the church, for a change in its attitude to artificial contraception. His successor was to be hagridden by the problem; John was not called on to tackle it. In his encyclicals he repeated, therefore, the conventional wisdom of moderate-minded Catholics of his day. The solution to the problem of poverty and overpopulation in the developing countries was "not to be found in expedients which attack human life at its very source" — that is, birth control and abortion. Of course, it was essential to divert much of the money now spent on armaments to alleviating hunger; he was "sick at heart" to witness the failure of the great powers to do so. But he did not accept that there was a fatal and growing imbalance between population and resources. Indeed, ". . . the resources which God in his goodness and wisdom has implanted in nature are well-nigh inexhaustible," and, moreover, God has given men the intelligence to discover means to exploit them indefinitely. Hence the real solution was "a renewed scientific and technical effort on man's part to deepen and extend his dominion over nature."

Would John have maintained the same attitude in the context of the seventies? It seems very unlikely. He had an instinct for the world's worries and enthusiasms, and tended to share them. If it had been put to him — so far as we know, no one dared to do so — that he was a little too inclined to go along with modish good causes, he would doubtless have replied that this was part of his job as pope. There was no such thing as the "ecological movement" in his day; had there been, he would almost certainly have sympathized with its anxieties, though, as a determined optimist, he would have rejected the doom theories of the extreme conservationists. Whether he would have changed the church's policy on artificial contraceptives is a much more difficult question to answer. He would, we may be sure, have handled the issue in a quite different spirit to that of Pope Paul VI, who removed the issue from the hands of the council, handed it to a team of experts, rejected their findings, and finally after much procrastination, during which the two sides had drawn themselves up in fierce battle array, opted for the conservative minority, thus ending with the worst of all possible worlds — an intransigeant doctrine and a disobedient church. John, by contrast, would have used his skill to prevent a polarization on the issue. He would never have allowed its solution to involve the central authority of the papacy, as Pope Paul unfortunately did. He would have aimed for the middle ground, perhaps basing the morality of artificial contraception on intention, rather than use *per se*. And, above all, he would have trusted the wisdom of the church fathers: this was quintessentially a problem that the council was designed, and supremely able, to resolve.

Indeed, in discussing John's policies, we have so far omitted the most important element in the means he devised for carrying them out. John trusted in Divine Providence. He thought he knew what needed to be done during his pontificate. But the renewal of the Catholic church which was central to his aims was not something to be carried through by the pope alone. It was a matter for the entire church, in the persons of its bishops. The pope, by his actions and conduct, by his speeches and encyclicals and personal contacts, had the duty to point the way, to inspire and encourage (occasionally warn), to set an example and, to some extent, lead and command. But, ultimately, it was the church in its collegiate capacity which had to take the decisions. In *Mater et Magistra*

John had made clear his view that secular states should operate on a constitutional basis. By summoning the Ecumenical Council he invited the Catholic church, also, to adopt the theory and practice of constitutionalism.

NINE

The New Pentecost

POPE JOHN'S GIFT for the simple but striking image was never better illustrated than on the occasions when he spoke of his Ecumenical Council. Its object, he once said, was "to restore the simple and pure lines which the face of Jesus's church wore at its birth." On another occasion, he compared the church to "the old village fountain whose waters gush forth for the people of today just as they have served countless generations in the past." There had been an interruption in the flow: the council's task was to ensure that all were abundantly served.

There is some disagreement on when the idea of the council first occurred to the pope. His secretary, Monsignor Capovilla, stated in an article published in the English Catholic weekly, *The Tablet,* on 4 September 1965, that he had considered the possibility of holding a council some time before he broached it to any of his curial colleagues. This is very likely: the notion of the collegiate church had been with him since the inception of his pontificate; it had been adumbrated in his decision to extend the conclave by one day, immediately after his election, to consult with the cardinals. But the actual decision was another matter. John was quite clear in his own mind that it was an inspiration, which he attributed to Divine Providence. He said so, on 27 February 1959, in a conversation with Antoine Wenger, editor of the French Catholic daily, *La Croix*. While in retreat before the actual opening of the council in 1962, he noted in his diary:

> Without any forethought I put forward in one of my first talks with my Secretary of State [Tardini], on 20 January 1959, the idea of an Ecumenical Council, a Diocesian Synod and the revision of the Code of Canon Law, all this being quite contrary to any previous supposition or idea of my own on this subject. I was the first to be surprised at my proposal, which was entirely my own idea.

According to John's own account, Cardinal Tardini's reception of the idea was enthusiastic: *"Si, si, un concilio!"* According to another account, hostile to John, Tardini thought the pope had gone "temporarily mad." At all events, Tardini's subsequent attitude to the council was not encouraging: he seems to have done his best to extend the period of preparation, and confidently predicted that it would take three years at least just to assemble the material for the preparatory commissions.

Moreover, when John raised the subject again five days later, in the presence of eighteen curial cardinals, their response was mute. He had chosen the occasion carefully. The prelates were assembled at Saint Paul's Outside the Walls at the end of Unity Octave. The culmination of a week's prayers for Christian unity seemed an appropriate time, the church built over the supposed tomb of the great internationalist apostle an appropriate place. But when John told the cardinals he intended to call a council, they said nothing. "It was only human nature," John wrote, "to have expected that the cardinals, after hearing our allocution, would have crowded round to express approval and good wishes." Instead, he recorded — putting the best construction on it — "there was a devoted and impressive silence. Explanations came on the following days." The consternation in the Curia was reflected in the peculiar manner which the *Osservatore Romano* chose to announce the momentous events in its next issue, 26–27 January. There were no blazing headlines, just a brief announcement that, in order to meet the errors of the time, and its excessive materialism, the pope intended to hold a synod of the Roman clergy, to call an ecumenical council of the universal church, and to modernize canon law; the council was also to be "an invitation to the separated communities to search for that unity towards which so many souls aspire." The news item, in fact, attempted both to downgrade the importance of John's decision to a level of triviality, and to invest it with a distorted and negative purpose — the repression of error and the condemnation of materialism — which was wholly alien to John's thinking.

Obviously, the curialists feared the idea of a council, both in the sense that, as bureaucrats, they resented innovation and in the sense that, as men who wielded power subject only to the pope's authority, they were disturbed by the intrusion of a new, and totally unknown, factor. Moreover, with some reason, they could argue that previous Ecumenical Councils had tended to promote discord rather than unity. Even John himself felt the need to point out, in his opening speech to the fathers, that councils had not always been able to ensure "the plenary triumph of the Christian idea and life, and the preservation of religious liberty." Indeed not. The first seven councils, held under the presidency of the Roman emperors, had on balance exacerbated the tensions between the Eastern and the Western churches. The medieval councils had failed either to establish the triumphalism they proclaimed or to produce the reforms in the church they acknowledged to be desirable. The great Council of Trent had confirmed, rather than healed, the split in the Western church. Vatican I, which had ended in confusion, had pushed the church further down the blind alley of Papal Infallibility without a corresponding definition of the role of the bishops. Few councils had concluded without subsequent anathemas and excommunications.

Beyond the Curia the reactions were mixed, at least initially. The French, never well disposed to ideas they have not originated, tended to take a cynical line. Pope John was *"pas serieux."* How could *un pape de passage* take the responsibility to initiate a train of events which would take years to unfold and might produce momentous consequences? Elsewhere, clergy and Catholic laity alike were first intrigued, then fascinated. And John was pleased and relieved that Cardinal Bea warmly welcomed the proposal, and had many suggestions to make. Cardinal Montini of Milan, whom John perhaps already saw as his possible successor, came out strongly in favor: "The Council will make Rome the spiritual capital of the world from whence the light will spread upon those places and institutions where men are working for the union of peoples, for the welfare of the poor, for progress, for justice and for liberty." This was exactly what John himself had in mind.

But, beyond this general aim, it is not clear whether John knew himself what precisely the council was to do, or even what form it should take. Was it to be an assembly of bishops of the Roman Catholic church, or a meeting of the Eastern and Western churches, or a universal gathering of all professing Christianity? Perhaps John, guided as he felt he was by Providence, thought these questions would resolve themselves in time, as indeed they did. Certainly, in the light of the brief *Osservatore* announcement, both the Orthodox and the Protestant churches supposed that the council would follow the pattern of Florence, in 1438, when 117 Latin bishops met thirty-one Greek-Orthodox patriarchs and bishops, in an unsuccessful attempt to end the schism. This may, indeed, have been John's intention: he left the first announcement of the council deliberately vague, to see what kind of response it would evoke from the Orthodox patriarchs. But this explanation is not very satisfactory. If it was his intention to include the Orthodox church, why had he not sounded out some at least of its senior figures before making any announcement at all? He knew, from long experience, the type of person with whom he was dealing. On the whole, it seems more likely that he thought an invitation to the Orthodox church would raise more problems than it solved and that, in the first instance at least, the council should be homogeneous. At any rate, on 4 April 1959, he clarified his intentions — or, as some would have it, rationalized his failure to provoke a response from Athens and Istanbul — by saying publicly that the unity shown by the forthcoming council "of the holy church of God" would itself "constitute an invitation to our separated brethren . . . to return to the universal flock . . ." This apparently marked the end of any attempt to include Orthodox clergy as full members of the council.

As for Protestants, who were regarded by Catholics not (like the Orthodox) as mere schismatics, but as heretics, there was never any real possibility that they would be invited to attend as delegates. Some of the Protestant churches had for many years established relationships with the Orthodox patriarchates. But this had been bitterly resented by the papacy, and all such jointly sponsored meetings had been forbidden to Catholics in the most vehement terms. The papacy had never denied the validity of Orthodox orders, or the claim of their bishops to the Apostolic Succession. But since the end of the sixteenth century it had refused to recognize either the Lutheran priesthood of Germany (still less the Calvinist ministry) or Anglican orders and their derivatives. As recently as 1896, Leo XIII's Bull, *Apostolicae Curae,* summing up years of supposed investigation and historical research, had pronounced Anglican orders as "absolutely null and utterly void" — a decision only recently (December 1973) reversed by implication. Successive popes had forbidden Catholics, clerical or lay, to participate in ecumenical gatherings attended by Protestants. This decision had been reinforced, after the abortive Malines Conversations, by Pius XI's encyclical *Mortalium Animos* in 1928; and in 1948–1949, instructions issued by the papal Holy Office (signed, it is interesting to note, by the future Cardinal Ottaviani, then one of its officials) had prohibited Catholics from attending meetings of the World Council of Churches.

Nevertheless, if in practice John was unable to include either Orthodox or Protestants as members of the council, he made persistent and resolute efforts to secure their attendance as observers. He wanted the council to be as universalist as possible. It is notable that, once the preparations got under way, he became increasingly convinced that both he, and it, had a world role to play. On 7 July 1959 he wrote in his diary: "We like to think that, in answer to our prayers, and to our sacrifices, Divine Providence is in the course of elucidating one of the greatest mysteries of history, the mystery of the mercy of the Lord for all peoples." Again, five months later, on 5 December: "All the world is my family. This sense of everybody belonging . . . This vision, this feeling of universality, shall henceforth enliven all my constant and uninterrupted daily prayers." In 1961 he hoped that the peoples would move together: ". . . the richer will help the poorer, the stronger will sustain the weaker, the more advanced will guide the less developed, and all will in the end feel themselves to be brothers because all are sons of the same very loving father who is in heaven."

This movement the pope would hasten by his example

and his actions, above all by doing everything in his power to bury ancient religious animosities. In Cardinal Bea he was beginning to discover an exceptionally able and enthusiastic lieutenant, of great experience in world affairs, and with a thorough grasp of the church's central and international machinery. It is true that Bea's vision was more limited than John's own. Where John thought in terms of all religions and peoples — Jews, Muslims and Buddhists, even men of no faith at all, as well as Christians of all denominations — Bea was primarily interested in the Christian context. That, indeed, was his job. His Secretariat for Christian Unity began its work in November 1960, with himself as president, and a Dutch ecclesiastical diplomat, Mgr. Jan Willibrands, as secretary. Under its terms of reference, it was to produce information for the other preparatory commissions and to pass on suggestions from what were now termed the "separated brethren"; it was also to explain the objects, and later the transactions, of the council to the other churches. In practice, however, its activities covered a much wider field, and with John's encouragement it began to function as an extra secretariat of state, taking initiatives and arranging contacts of a kind which traditional Vatican diplomacy had always avoided. Bea, in particular, acquired John's complete confidence and was allowed almost total freedom of action. He traveled constantly, thus giving (as the Romans put it) a new meaning to the slogan of British Airways — "See the World with BEA." Monsignor Willibrands was sent to the meeting of the Central Committee of the World Council of Churches — hitherto scornfully boycotted by the Vatican — in August

1960, and arranged for a group of Catholic theologians to attend, as observers, the Assembly of the World Council at New Delhi in November 1961. The secretariat was staffed mainly by Catholic priests from predominantly Protestant countries, who were used to dealing with non-Catholic Christians. It did not take doctrinal initiatives, but it acquired a body of knowledge about the details and attitudes which separated the different churches, and this was to prove invaluable when the council met. It also developed personal friendships and so promoted an atmosphere in which, for the first time, it became normal and natural for Christian theologians to discuss their differences in a relaxed manner. In November 1960, Archbishop Fisher paid a call on the pope: not since the beginning of the Reformation had the successor of Saint Augustine of Canterbury met the successor of Saint Peter.

Contacts with the Orthodox hierarchy proved much more difficult to establish, not through any lack of enthusiasm on the part of the Vatican but because of ancient divisions in the Orthodox church itself. This came as no surprise to John, who was familiar with the mutual jealousies between Athens and Constantinople, and between both and the patriarchate of Moscow, which they regarded as a department of the Soviet government. John could invite all three separately, and risk offending the "free" patriarchates; or he could issue a general invitation, and leave the Orthodox churches themselves to work out how they would be represented. He decided on the second course, but met with no response. For this, Athens's deep-rooted suspicions of Rome were chiefly responsible. On October 8, three days before the council opened, Cardinal Bea, after many inquiries, at last got a message from Patriarch Athenagoras of Constantinople (Istanbul) informing him that it was impossible to send observers: he could not get a positive reply from Moscow and Athens had been openly discouraging. Meanwhile, it had become clear that Moscow's silence was diplomatic: its patriarchate, or perhaps the Soviet government, expected a separate invitation, and not one transmitted through Constantinople. When John realized this, he decided to change his policy. Monsignor Willibrands was sent to Moscow, on 27 September 1962, with an invitation in his pocket, and the next week the Kremlin agreed to allow two official Orthodox observers to attend — the only ones to do so. The news came as an unpleasant surprise to the other Orthodox patriarchates, and Athens was quick to accuse the Vatican of duplicity. It is true that John might have handled the affair more skillfully. But there was certainly no desire on his part to exploit the divisions in the Orthodox churches: he was, and remained, anxious to have them all present. Evidently, Athenagoras of Constantinople, at least, came to accept that John had acted in good faith, and later, after John's death, he had a successful meeting with Pope Paul VI in Jerusalem. But for the first session of the council, at any rate on an official basis, Moscow alone represented the Orthodox camp, in the shape of the Archpriest Vitali Borovoi and the Archimandrite Vladimir Kotlyarov.

From this episode, it was clear that the Soviet government had decided to adopt a benevolent attitude towards the council. Mr. Khrushchev felt that Pope John's world diplomacy could be turned to advantage in pursuing his own policy of "peaceful coexistence." Private assurances were given to him that the council would not be used as an anti-Communist platform, and it therefore became in his interest to secure representation from countries controlled by the Soviet bloc. This, of course, covered a much wider field than the issue of Orthodox observers from Moscow. Pope John, naturally, wanted the Catholic bishops from the "church of silence" to attend. But he was not very optimistic. In 1869, as he liked to point out to professional anti-Communists, the czarist government had flatly refused permission to the Polish bishops to attend the First Vatican Council: most of Poland was then incorporated in the Russian state, and St. Petersburg feared that the Poles would use the council to make anti-Russian propaganda. Russian imperialist policy had not changed substantially in the meantime. John, therefore, was agreeably surprised when it became apparent that a large number of Catholic bishops would be allowed to cross the Iron Curtain. In the event, for the first session, Cardinal Stefan Wyszynski of Warsaw and sixteen other bishops came from Poland, four from East Germany, three from Hungary, three from Czechoslovakia, and the full contingent of Yugoslav bishops. John met with failure in Rumania and Albania, states which prided themselves on their independence of the Moscow "line"; and most of the Catholic bishops of mainland China were in prison.

There was nothing John could do about China, but he took advantage of Moscow's benevolence to try to secure the release of various prelates held in captivity in the Soviet sphere of influence for alleged war crimes.

After the opening of the council, he began secret negotiations over the case of Mgr. Josef Slipyi, the Catholic
archbishop of the Byzantine rite in Lvov, now classified
as part of the Ukraine, who had been held in jail for
seventeen years. One of the intermediaries was the American Norman Cousins, editor of the *Saturday Review,*
who saw Mr. Khrushchev in December 1962 and, with
John's previous agreement, raised the Slipyi case. Khrushchev said he did not know whether the archbishop was
still alive, but would look into it. Some weeks later, in
Washington, Cousins was told by the Soviet ambassador
that the archbishop was being released unconditionally,
and that it was now for the Vatican to decide where he
should live. John was at supper when the news reached
him by telephone. He thought this an excellent excuse
to break his diet, and called for a bottle of wine to drink
Monsignor Slipyi's health. Monsignor Willibrands was
dispatched to Moscow to bring the archbishop to Rome,
and the old prelate was joyfully received by the pope on
10 February 1963. The release of Slipyi was the most
sensational personal triumph of John's Iron Curtain
diplomacy, but there were others, some of which did not
mature until after his death. Thus, Cardinal Koenig of
Vienna was allowed to visit Cardinal Mindszenty in his
sanctuary at the United States embassy in Budapest, and
begin a series of conversations which eventually led to
his arrival in Rome; and John also took up the case of
Mgr. Josef Beran, archbishop of Prague, who had been
under restriction since 1947. Monsignor Beran had his
liberty fully restored in 1964, when he was allowed to go
to Rome to receive his cardinal's hat from Pope Paul VI.

There were other ways in which the initiatives taken by Pope John produced a lightening of the burden on the "church of silence." Indeed, his policy of *rapprochement* with the Communist world was far more effective in improving conditions for Catholics behind the Iron Curtain than the continuous and hostile propaganda warfare waged by the Vatican before his accession.

In terms of the council, however, Pope John was even more anxious to secure the approbation, and the endorsement, of the non-Catholic Christian world. He rightly forecast that its presence, in strength, at the sessions would act as an ecumenical force on the assembled Catholic bishops. Despite the difficulties with the Orthodox churches, Bea's efforts, on the whole, were remarkably successful. When the council met, there were more than forty "observers," in addition to the two official representatives from Moscow. They included accredited delegations from the Coptic church of Egypt, the Syrian Orthodox church, the Ethiopian church, the Armenian church, and the Russian Orthodox church in exile. There were also official representatives of the Old Catholics, the Anglicans, the Lutherans, the Calvinists, the Congregationalists, the Methodists, the Quakers, the Disciples of Christ, the Taize Community, and the secretariat of the World Council of Churches, delegated by many lesser denominations. Halfway through the first session, Bishop Cassien arrived as an unofficial delegate of the Orthodox church, and many representatives, especially from the Orthodox world, attended the later sessions, so that the observer group eventually numbered over a hundred.

The overall success of the operation is attested by Dr.

John Moorman, bishop of Ripon and senior Anglican observer, whose little book on the council is perhaps the best account of it from a Protestant viewpoint. Dr. Moorman complains that the limitations imposed on the participation of observers by the traditionalists in the Curia limited their usefulness. None of them expected to be allowed to vote, but it was a disappointment that they were never allowed to address the council, or even to give public thanks for their considerate treatment. Nor were any of them officially consulted by the various commissions, though on a number of topics discussed by the council — clerical marriage, communion in both kinds, the role of the diaconate, and the vernacular liturgy, for example — where the Catholic church was treading new ground, the observers had much to teach. On the other hand, they were allowed to attend all the debates; indeed, John and Bea had arranged to give them better seats than any of the bishops. Through private contacts, and especially through the Unity Secretariat, they exerted considerable influence behind the scenes. And, perhaps equally important, their very presence acted as a restraining influence on religious bigotry during the debates. The triumphalist rhetoric which had been so baneful a feature of the First Vatican Council was conspicuously absent, in part at least because even the curialists knew their words were being noted by intelligent and sympathetic experts of other faiths, and modified their language accordingly. As Dr. Moorman points out, speakers whose remarks were ill-received in the observers' tribunal were liable to find themselves publicly rebuked by later speakers; and he relates that, at the end of the first session,

Monsignor Willibrands said to him: "The presence of the observers here is very important. You have no idea how much they are influencing the work of the Council." Moreover, after the experience gained at the first session, and the friendships established, the observers influenced later sessions more directly, by getting sympathetic bishops to raise points and advance arguments they would have put themselves had they been allowed to speak. As an exercise in ecumenicalism, the council proved a notable success, though more for what it set in motion than for what it accomplished.

While Pope John and Cardinal Bea had been working to secure the widest possible representation at the council, a long and sometimes acrimonious battle was being fought over its agenda, or to be precise over the preparatory documents, or *schemata,* to be submitted to it. On the feast of Pentecost, in 1959, John set up what was termed an Ante-Preparatory Commission, under the presidency of Cardinal Tardini, to solicit suggestions from dioceses all over the world, and from religious orders, about the ground the council should cover, and the direction it should take. A year later, having examined over 2,000 suggested agendas, it reported to John, and on the basis of its findings he set up eleven preparatory commissions to draft the actual schemata. They began their work on 13 November 1960, twelve days before John celebrated his seventy-ninth birthday, and twenty-two months after he had announced the summoning of the council. Much time, therefore, had already elapsed, and John was increasingly anxious to hurry on the procedure. He brushed aside Tardini's insistence that at least three years would be needed to prepare the schemata, and cut it down to less than two; indeed, on every occasion when the curialists pressed him to extend the preparatory period, he responded by shortening it. Finally, on the feast of Candlemas, 2 February 1962, he issued a *Moto Proprio* definitely fixing the opening date of the council for 11 October. The speech in which he made this announcement, with its characteristic reference to the liturgy of the day, made it clear that he wished to make the council ecumenical, indeed universalist, in spirit even if only Catholics composed it:

> Jesus is the redeemer of the whole human race. Today he is saluted as "a light to lighten the nations," the saviour of all the nations. To him, therefore, belong not only all those who are sons of the Catholic Church, but all those who are baptised in his holy name, and also all those who are equally his by right of creation and by the saving virtue of his precious blood, shed for the salvation of the whole human race. . . . May this redeeming blood fall upon all men, become no longer strangers or enemies but brothers. May it strengthen their will for peace, their longing after tranquillity and well-being.

The first line of defense of the curialists had been to delay the opening of the council, in the hope that John would have disappeared before it met, and that his successor would have second thoughts. This was broken by the Candlemas announcement. Their second line of defense, which at one time looked as though it might succeed, was to turn the council into a rubber stamp by hurrying it into monolithic votes on documents prepared, in effect, by the Curia itself. To some extent John's pre-council strategy played into their hands. The territory covered by the eleven preparatory commissions followed roughly the pattern of the Vatican's own ministerial departments — Theology, Bishops and Government, Discipline, Religious Orders, the Sacraments, the Liturgy, Studies and Seminaries, the Oriental Churches, the Missions, the Laity, and Ceremonial. John, who appointed the members of the commissions, placed each under the presidency of the cardinal who controlled the corresponding department of the Curia. It is true that John said quite specifically that it was not his wish that council matters should be controlled by the Curia: "The government of the church, which is the occupation of the Curia, is one thing, and the Council is another." But in practice the presidents of the commissions controlled the timing, duration and agendas of their meetings, drew up the drafts for discussions, decided which outside experts were to be called in (or not), and steered their discussions to conclusions which had been preordained in secret curial planning sessions. The only preparatory bodies effectively dominated by men who supported the spirit of the council were the Central Steering Commission, presided over by John himself, and Bea's Unity Secretariat. Bea's secretariat was specifically commanded to work with all the commissions, when relevant. In fact it was unable to do so. Its proposals or suggestions were pigeonholed or flatly rejected. One important instance of this was publicly revealed during the opening session by Mgr. Emile de Smedt, the bishop of Bruges, who worked on the Unity Secretariat. He said that, despite the pope's command that the secretariat should help the commissions to prepare the drafts of the schemata "in a truly ecumenical way," Cardinal Ottaviani, president of the key Theological Commission, had twice declined their offers of assistance. "I am sorry to have to say so," he added, "but it is the simple truth" (he might also have pointed out that his statement flatly contradicted an assertion by Ottaviani that he had carried out the pope's wishes).

John had a good idea what the Curia was up to, since in June 1962 there was a blazing row on his own Central Commission (he was not normally present at its meetings), when Ottaviani tried to impose a ban on the issue of a pastoral letter about the council which had been drafted by the Dutch episcopate. He was hotly opposed by Cardinals Alfrink of Utrecht, Doepfner of Munich, Koenig of Vienna and Lienart of Lille, who won their point. Ottaviani was incensed by a remark of Cardinal Gracias of Bombay, who pointed out that, though councils usually ended by somebody being forced into schism, or heresy, this time it would not be the "outsiders" like himself, since they were in a majority. In the angry discussion which followed, the fighting word "freemasons" was flung at the curialists. When John was told about the row, he summoned the leading protagonists and told them to calm down.

Actually, "freemasonry" was not a bad description for the way the curialists operated. Though they held most of the key posts, and dominated the preparatory work, they also met among themselves privately and coordinated their tactics. The commissions mirrored the Curia; and the Curia, in the phrase of Xavier Rynne, the best informed historian of the council, is "controlled by an interlocking directorate of bishops and monsignors, all Italian." These men, comparatively few in number, were pluralists on the grandest scale. Rynne cites the case of Archbishop Pietro Parente, who, among other things, was administrative director of the Holy Office, consultor of the Consistorial Congregation (which nominates and supervises bishops), a member of the Congregation of the Council (discipline of clergy), consultor of the Congregation of the Propagation of the Faith (missions), a member of the Congregation of Rites, of the Commission for Latin America, and of the Commission for Cinema, Radio and TV. Parente was an example of how the freemasonry operated, since during his career he had contrived to anger Pius XI (who expelled him from Rome) and the archdiocese of Perugia (from which he was removed in 1959); nevertheless, thanks to his friends, he not only survived but contrived to exert more influence on the appointments to the council commissions than any other official, with the one exception of Archbishop Pericle Felici, the secretary-general of the council, who was another member of the curial freemasonry. Moreover, in the preparatory work, the curialists were successful not only in including their supporters, but in excluding those they regarded as dangerous. In preparing the schemata, over 800 bishops and theologians were consulted by the commissions. But a number of leading progressive theologians were deliberately ignored (or consulted at the last moment, under pressure). These included John Courtney Murray S.J. and John L. McKenzie from the United States, Henri de Lubac, M-D Chenu and Jean Danielou S.J. from France, and Karl Rahner from Austria.

Why did Pope John decline to take measures to curb the influence of the curial freemasonry and frustrate its attempt to rig the council's work? It may be that, while aware of some backstage bickerings, he underestimated the extent of the Curia's activities, and was deeply shocked when he finally discovered the depth of curial opposition to the purpose of his council. John preferred to take an optimistic view of men's motives: on the whole he found that it tended to disarm opponents. Then, too, John always showed himself anxious to work through the Curia, whenever possible, in the hope that he could carry it along with him; again, this hope was not always naive. But, above all, John trusted in Providence, and the power of the Holy Spirit working through the council itself. He rightly guessed that 2,500 bishops, representing the entire Catholic world of 600 million souls, would prove more than a match for the Curia, once the fathers got to know their power. And, therefore, it was best to allow the curialists to work confidently away, and show their hand when the council met. Then the council could defeat them in the open, where they were most vulnerable. If he drove the curialist opposition underground, it would certainly reorganize itself and might prove more effective as a guerrilla force. Naturally, John did not reason in precisely these military terms. But it is clear enough that he thought the council should be put to the test, and taught to win its own battles: that was part of the process by which, he hoped, the collegiate spirit of the episcopate would come to play its full part in the government of the church.

However, John felt it right that he should give the

council fathers an unmistakable lead, and he prepared the opening ceremony with particular care. As a rule, he used to go into retreat in the first week of December. In 1962, however, immediately after his return from Castel Gandolfo, at the beginning of September, he made a seven-day retreat in a curious hideout he had made for himself in the Vatican. This was the old Tower of Saint John, built into the Vatican walls, near the Porta Pertusa. Until 1961 it had been dominated by a gigantic and hideous metal mast used by Vatican Radio. John had the mast removed, the tower raised to a height of seven stories, and installed a residential suite for himself, together with a kitchen and servants' quarters. Here he was completely cut off from the world. Except in emergencies, only three people had access to him: Monsignor Capovilla, his secretary, Bishop Cavagna, his confessor, and his Latin tutor, Father Ciappi. John spent a good deal of time writing, interrupting himself from time to time to pray at his favorite Vatican grotto, the statue of the Madonna of Massabielle, which he could reach directly from his tower by a private covered way which he had had built through the Walls of Nicholas V. In the Tower of Saint John, the pope composed his opening speech, which seems to have been inspired, or rather provoked, by a remarkable lecture given at the Lateran University in the autumn of 1960, by Cardinal Pizzardo. Pizzardo had been Ottaviani's superior, and mentor, at the Holy Office, and in his day he had been considered the most important member of the Curia *Pentegone*. In his attitude to the world, he represented the defensive, isolationist spirit of the late pope, the credo of a church dominated by fear, which John was trying to reform. Pizzardo may have been angered by some of John's initiatives, and felt that it was time for the Old Guard to speak out. At all events, in his lecture he made his feelings perfectly clear, and in very colorful language. It was nonsense, he said, to think of one world. There were two worlds confronting mankind: the so-called modern world, which was the City of Satan, and the City of God, symbolized and represented by the Vatican. The world beyond the walls of the Vatican City was "the new city of Babel. It rises on a basis of crude materialism and blind determinism, built by the unconscious toil of the conquered, and bathed in their tears and blood, like the old pagan Colosseum — a ruin washed over by the Christian centuries. It rises up monstrous, holding out before the eyes of the deluded mob of slaves — bringing bricks and pitch for its making — a vain mirage of perfect prosperity and terrestrial felicity. . . . But at the same time on the glacis of the New Babel, there arise the launching ramps for missiles, and in its storehouse the ogival nuclear weapons pile up for the universal and total destruction to come."

Pope John evidently brooded on this impressive outburst. It seemed to him to express perfectly the negative, apprehensive and essentially defensive outlook against which he was striving. In its concept of a tiny and glorious elite struggling against a world of darkness, it was almost Calvinist. In its prognostication of disaster it was not only misguided but had, even in the recent past, been demonstrably mistaken: had not the loss of the papal states, regarded by successive popes as an unmitigated catastro-

phe, come to be recognized as a blessing in disguise? Had
not Providence been shown, time and again, to be more
worthy of trust than the apocalyptics? Were they not men
of little faith? Above all, if change was to be feared and
shunned as intrinsically evil, how could the church fulfill
its mission, which was, with God's grace, to save the entire world? John decided to make a considered reply to
Pizzardo's anathema of the universe. He could not match
its rhetoric, but he could make his own views unmistakably clear. A month before the council assembled, on 11
September, he made a public address to the world on
Vatican Radio, in which he gently indicated what he
considered to be its objects: it should concern itself with
the entire human race, and its right to freedom, justice
and the good life. His thunders, and his positive declaration of his own optimism, he reserved for the opening
day, to be given direct to the fathers themselves. The
ceremonial inauguration was dramatic: no such gathering
of senior clergy had been seen before in world history,
and the great Basilica of Saint Peter's made a spectacular
setting. Mass was said in both Latin and Greek, and in
all the opening service lasted five and a half hours, from
8 A.M. to 1:30 P.M.: it is set out in meticulous detail
in the official manual: *Methodus servanda et preces reci-
tandae in Concilio Oecumenico Vaticano II.* Pope John,
who was present throughout, and who was now eighty-
one, had cunningly taken precautions against hunger and
exhaustion. One of the diplomatic observers, Sir d'Arcy
Osborne, recorded that, halfway through, he contrived to
take a cup of coffee and a sandwich behind a scarlet
screen of cardinal-deacons. He needed to conserve his

strength for his opening address. And, when the moment
came, his deep voice was powerful and confident. He
scorned the pessimists. He exhorted the fathers to adopt
a spirit of adventure, and seize the opportunities Providence had given them:

> We are shocked to discover what is being said by some
> people who, though they may be fired by religious zeal,
> are without justice, or good judgment, or consideration
> in their way of looking at matters. In the existing state
> of society they see nothing but ruin and calamity. They
> are in the habit of saying that our age is much worse than
> past centuries. They behave as though history, which
> teaches us about life, has nothing to teach them. They
> behave as though, at the times of past councils, every-
> thing was perfect in the state of doctrine of the Christian
> church, in the behaviour of the faithful, and in the free-
> dom of action which the church enjoyed. It seems to us
> necessary to express our complete disagreement with
> these prophets of doom (*rerum adversarum vaticina-*
> *tores*), who give us news only of catastrophes, as though
> the world were nearing its end (*qui deteriora semper*
> *praenunciant, quasi rerum exitium instet*). . . . On the
> contrary, we should recognise that, at the present histor-
> ical moment, Divine Providence is leading us towards a
> new order in human relationships, which, through the
> agency of men and, what is more, above and beyond
> their own expectations, are tending towards the fulfil-
> ment of higher and, as yet, mysterious and unforeseen
> designs. Everything, even those events which seem to con-
> flict with her purposes, is ordered for the greater well-
> being of the church.

It was a trumpet call. Many of those present to hear
it, not yet accustomed to Latin spoken in a strong Italian

accent, and the cadences of Vatican prose, did not at first fully grasp its meaning. But a study of the brief text soon left no one in any doubt that Pope John had asked the council to assert itself. No absolute monarch, opening the first constitutional assembly, could have issued a more generous invitation. Now it was up to the bishops.

TEN

Sources of Authority

It MAY BE that Pope John will go down in history as a great propagandist, if a high-minded one. Certainly, by holding the council, he focused worldwide attention on the Catholic church and its doings in a way never before seen in living memory. One of those present, Peter Nichols of the London *Times*, calculated that over 3,000 journalists were regularly accredited to the council. In addition to the 2,500 cardinals, patriarchs, bishops and heads of religious orders, and their staffs, many thousands of clerical "experts," hangers-on and busybodies congregated in Rome. It was said that John's prohibition on the clergy attending public spectacles in the Rome diocese had been timely: with so many priests in the capital, no one else would have been able to get in. The astonishing variety of clerical garb, the multiplicity of tongues, of races, of colors, brought home to the world, who watched the public proceedings on TV, the genuine cosmopolitanism of the church. Latin briefly revived itself as a language of commerce. The *Osservatore* carried advertisements from car rental firms: "*novae automobiles quacumque amplitudine omnibusque numeris absolutae etiam sine raeario*"; and banks: "*peculiarem mensam argentariam apud additiciam procurationis sedem quae eorum necessitatibus inserviat.*" Rome became once more, as it had been before the foundation of the Italian state, an ecclesiastical capital whose business was religion.

With the eyes of the world on the council, and with his own diplomatic offensive under way (*Pacem in Terris* was ready for publication at a suitable moment), John was anxious both to exclude any political recriminations from the council's debates, and any attempt at political interference in its work by secular governments — as had, indeed, happened at every previous council. Insofar as the council was a political, as well as an ecclesiastical, act, its sole concern, he argued, must be with universal peace: that was its message. It was a matter of great grief to him that the word "peace," as a result of Soviet "peace campaigns," and the fierce opposition they had aroused, had become a dirty word. "We have even reached the point," he said, "of abusing that sweet word peace." His object was to cleanse it, to make it shine again in men's eyes as the noblest word of all. In his opening address to the council he had pointed the direction he hoped it would take. On the following day, in his last public act before the council got under way, he gave a short talk to the heads of eighty-six diplomatic missions in the Sistine Chapel. He wanted to make it clear to them that the council was universalist and nonpartisan. He made no reference to the "church of silence": it was a phrase he had dismissed from his vocabulary. The church was not silent, and its message was peace. He pointed to the magnificent panorama of Michelangelo's *Last Judgment:* all governments, he said, like all men and women, would one day have to render their account to the Supreme Judge. He added:

> Let all who bear the responsibility of government hear the anguished cry which, from every part of the world, from innocent children to old men, from individuals and from communities, rises to heaven: peace, peace. May the thought that they will have to render their own account prevent them from ever neglecting any opportunity to achieve that good which, for the human family, is the highest good of all.

John had already arranged to submit to the council, for its approval, the draft of a "message from the Council to Mankind." This had originally been suggested by two French Dominican theologians, Fathers Chenu and Yyes Congar, and had been framed deliberately on a non-religious basis on natural morality, suitable for a secular audience. But a text which did not mention the Deity was considered inappropriate for a council to issue, and the document was completely rewritten, at John's request, by a team of four French bishops, and tabled in his own name. It came before the council on 20 October, and was debated at length. Monsignor Fiordelli, bishop of Prato, objected that it contained no reference to the plight of Christians behind the Iron Curtain; but the Iron Curtain bishops felt this would do more harm than good, and the proposal was dropped. For this reason, the Ukrainian bishops in exile (their leader, Archbishop Slipyi, was then still in prison) voted against it, and issued a minority statement of their own. The text then went through, with the addition of a reference to the Virgin Mary. It drew attention to God's love for all mankind, which it was the church's duty to express by its constant solicitude for the material, as well as the spiritual, welfare of all the peoples: and it had the joy and privilege of delivering to the world the "good news," as the Bible put it, that all could be saved. Though French in inspiration, the document as it emerged was a simple little Johannine homily, which had the additional merit of defusing any possible explosion of international issues during the debates. John, indeed, was becoming increasingly worried by the international situation, as the council got into its stride. A week after it opened, the Cuban missile crisis burst upon the world, and for several days there was a real possibility of a thermonuclear war. On 25 October, Pope John issued an appeal to the world: its language was deliberately neutral, but the tone in which it pleaded for a negotiated settlement was passionate.

By this time, John had withdrawn from the council, as he had always intended. It was essentially a parliament of the episcopate. As a constitutional monarch, he had summoned it, he had opened it, he had given it advice and encouragement, and he would close it. He held himself in reserve to intervene if necessary. But its work was bishops' work, not his. Of course, he followed the debates constantly, for the most part watching them on closed-circuit TV installed in his quarters. He was absorbed by the personalities as well as the issues. It was very characteristic both of his compassion, and of his interests, that he intervened in the case of Bishop Petar Cule of Mostar in Yugoslavia. Monsignor Cule, in the debate on the liturgy, was anxious that a reference to Saint Joseph be inserted in the Canon of the mass. It was a perfectly proper point to put forward — one, as a matter of fact, which appealed strongly to John himself. But the bishop was nervous, and rambled on, and the fathers grew restive. Cardinal Ruffini of Palermo, who was presiding, cut the bishop short (ten minutes was the maximum for speakers from the floor) in what many felt was an uncharitable manner: "Complete your holy and eloquent speech. We all love Saint Joseph, and we hope there are many saints in Yugoslavia." This raised a laugh, but John was not amused. Unlike the overwhelming majority of those present, and no doubt Ruffini himself, he knew that Bishop Cule had suffered appalling ill-treatment during the war, and that his hesitant manner reflected his sufferings. Being John, he did not rebuke Ruffini; he simply, on his own authority, inserted Saint Joseph's name in the Canon, and published the fact three days later. For the bishop, the little incident was an unexpected triumph; for John, a cause of satisfaction — sometimes it was an agreeable privilege to be pope.

However, as pope, he had to leave the bishops as a whole to fight their own battles. That, indeed, was one of the functions of the council: to educate them in constitutional politics. They had to learn how to come to terms with the Curia. John did not want reform to be imposed from above, or to surge up from below, as it had done at the Reformation, but to emerge from the church as a whole, acting together: *ut unam sint* (let them be one) was a phrase he repeated often. This was one reason why he did not wish to curb the Curia himself: the bishops must do it. They must develop the habit of thinking for themselves, and, equally important, of learning to act in concert. It is a curious fact that, until the council, the Italian bishops, for instance, had never met before in a body. In some other countries there were regular episcopal conferences to discuss policy and action. One object of the council, therefore, was for the bishops of one country to learn from the bishops of another; and, equally, to educate the more stolid elements among the episcopate by bringing them into contact with more agile-minded and progressive bishops from elsewhere. John had set in motion a fermenting process, and now he could sit by his TV set and watch it work.

The curialists had prepared the ground carefully for a rubber-stamp assembly. In the first place they controlled the press outlets, that is, not only the Vatican newspapers but the special press office set up to publish summaries of the council's doings (the press, of course, was excluded from the debates). John himself was well disposed to the press, and anxious that it should have full access to conciliar news; so were his secretary, Capovilla, his assistant for protocol, Igino Cardinale (later apostolic delegate in Britain) and, with his American training, the secretary of state, Cardinal Cicognani. But the press office itself was under the control of Monsignor Vallainc, a priest from the Val d'Aosta, a man of much experience in journalism (he had run a Catholic news agency) but little technical competence and no imagination. He was a typical Curia pluralist, who had accumulated an extraordinary range of appointments on the public relations side of the Vatican and therefore, it was argued by his friends, was a "natural" choice to control the council's press outlets. But he had been brought up in a school which regarded the secular press with suspicion if not downright hostility, and which conceived it the duty of clerical press officers to deny or manage information, rather than to provide it. Vallainc proved himself courteous and friendly, but not a dispenser of news. He was allowed, ex officio, to attend the meetings of the Central Preparatory Commission, but communicated little of its doings to reporters. Again, ex officio, he sat in the council as an "expert." But he had taken the conciliar oath to preserve its secrets, and interpreted the oath literally. Indeed, it was said that Monsignor Vallainc was the only member of the council who never divulged its secrets. The council press office, in fact, proved of very little value to journalists. What the curialist public-relations clergy did do, however, was to present a tendentious version of events through the official Vatican organs. This proved counterproductive. The world press quickly learned to distrust the Vatican papers, and, deprived of normal sources of information through official briefings, made their own contacts with the council fathers. Gradually, the veil of secrecy was lifted by, as it were, private enterprise. The truth came out, first in driblets, then, increasingly, in a steady stream; and by the end of the first session, entire speeches and accurate summaries of debates were circulating. From the curialists' viewpoint, they would have been better advised to treat the press to full disclosure. Indeed, it would have been more sensible for all concerned if the press had been present at the debates. As it was, the progressives won the press battle hands down: it was essentially their version of events which was communicated to the world. The various unofficial attempts, by the conservatives, to influence opinion proved disastrous. "Lo Svizzero," the pseudonymous Vatican correspondent of the extreme right-wing weekly, *Il Borghese*, published an attack on both Pope John and the council, under the title *La Chiesa dopo Giovanni;* another attack, in less restrained language, though again under a pseudonym, "Maurice Pinay," appeared in a book called *Complotto contro la Chiesa;* and a scurrilous anti-Semitic tract, circulated outside Saint Peter's (by, it was said, a group of clerics which included junior Vatican officials), attempted to present the council as an anti-Catholic Jewish conspiracy, resurrecting such hoary myths as the "Protocols of Zion." These efforts, whoever sponsored them, did the curialists much more harm than good. In any case, it soon became perfectly simple for any hard-working journalist to discover exactly what was being said in the basilica.

This was important, not least for the council fathers themselves, some of whom found it difficult to follow the Latin debates. The curialists may have believed that the compulsory use of Latin favored them: on the whole, they were accustomed to it, and the "outsiders" were not. It certainly made debating, as opposed to a series of prepared, and often unrelated, speeches difficult. Speakers usually lacked the skill to deal impromptu with points raised in the discussions. But for the curialists, their greater familiarity with church Latin was a diminishing asset as the council proceeded. Indeed, some of the progressive spokesmen proved themselves masters of the language. On the whole, compulsory Latin was a neutral force. But it caused a great deal of trouble, and often confusion. Sometimes the texts of motions were imperfectly understood, and bishops found afterwards that they had voted in the wrong lobby. Sometimes what they thought they had said was turned upside down. Thus, Cardinal Godfrey, the extremely conservative archbishop of Westminster, made a speech hotly defending the use of Latin in the liturgy, and used the words *"debemus levare linguam latinam." Levare* in Italian means to throw away, not raise up, and *Il Tiempo* reported the cardinal as insisting that Latin be abolished. Perhaps the most important consequence of the insistence on Latin was to emasculate the influence of the huge and powerful contingent of bishops from the United States. There were notable exceptions, but few of the Americans were able to take their rightful place in the debates. Cardinal Spellman of New York found it necessary to speak through a *narator,* since few could understand his brand of Latin. The vigorous and strong-minded Cardinal Cushing of Boston openly confessed he could not cope, and this was the reason why he played so small a part in the council. Only one man, the eighty-four-year-old Maximos IV Saigh, Melchite Patriarch of Antioch, openly flouted the rules and spoke in French. He made himself very popular, and it was unfortunate more did not follow his example.

The curialists had hoped that the use of Latin, insofar as it restricted and inhibited debate, would make it easier for them to manage the council. They placed great faith in their control of procedure. It was they, by the dominance of the preparatory commissions, who were in effect presenting a series of bills to the fathers. It was in their interests to turn the debates into perfunctory exercises, and hurry up the voting on preordained motions. Bishops who did not agree would then be placed in the position of appearing to impede the will of the council as a whole. Then the council would get through its business before the anticurial opposition had time to organize itself. This, to a great extent, was what happened at the First Vatican Council. But there was one snag. The Curia had wanted a fixed agenda. Pope John decided otherwise: it was for the council to determine how to conduct its business. Thus the curialists' vision of a bureaucratic steamroller, advancing remorselessly and crushing opposition according to a prearranged timetable, was replaced by something much closer to an open forum, in which debates could be prolonged, or curtailed, or advanced or postponed, and in which the bishops, rather than the council secretariat, held the advantage. Moreover, and this was far more important, the curialists soon discovered that the progressives were far more adept than they at parliamentary business, as indeed might have been expected. In brainpower and in sheer tactical skills, the bureaucrats were heavily outmatched.

This became apparent on the first day that the council got down to business, Saturday 13 October. Cardinal Ottaviani had assumed that the members of the preparatory commissions, which the Curia controlled, would simply be confirmed as members of the actual conciliar commissions, and could then steer their texts through unamended and, he hoped, virtually unopposed. He introduced a motion to this effect. To his consternation, Cardinal Lienart of Lille immediately rose to object to the motion. The elections to the commissions, he proposed, should be delayed until regional and national episcopal conferences had had the opportunity to meet and agree on candidates. He was seconded, clearly by prearrangement, by Cardinal Frings of Cologne. The curialists were taken aback by the evident degree of preparation among their opponents, and in their confusion Lienart's motion was carried without a vote. Thus the huge advantage the curialists had patiently acquired on the commissions, during the years of preparation, was lost at a stroke. Moreover, the emergence of episcopal conferences, at the very outset of the council, meant that the curialists were now faced, before they had got a single text through, not by individual but by collective, and organized, opposition. What was equally significant was that the council then proceeded to enact that, to save endless balloting, candidates should be elected not by two-thirds majorities, as the council rules provided, but by simple majorities. They appealed to the pope to suspend the two-thirds rule in this case, and, as they clearly expressed the will of the majority, he agreed. The curialists had been counting on the two-thirds rule as a protective fallback position, should the majority of the council go against them. If they could not win, they felt they could probably muster enough votes to block their opponents. Now an important precedent had been set, not merely for suspending the rule, but for papal intervention at the behest of the majority.

The central business of the council began on 22 October, with the opening of the debate on the *schema* dealing with the liturgy. Here, paradoxically, the progressives stood at a procedural advantage, for many aspects of the liturgical schema were congenial to them, and the curialists were thus obliged to be critical of the first conciliar document, although their general strategy was to create an atmosphere in which all prepared schemata would go through on the nod. It is possible that they had planned to offer the liturgical schema, which did contain modernistic elements, as a sop to the progressives, in the hope that the council would begin with an apparent concession to change, and so allow the much more vital (to them) schema on the Sources of Revelation, which was wholly conservative, to be accepted without much debate. But they had engaged in jiggery-pokery at the last minute. The liturgical schema, as actually presented to the council, had been altered by the secretariat in two important respects: sections dealing with the biblical foundations of the liturgy had been suppressed, and a section had been inserted stating that the schema laid down only general principles, whose application was to be determined solely by the Holy See (that is, in practice, the Curia). This was at once pointed out, notably by Cardinals Frings and Doepfner, and a long debate followed, not merely on the nature of the liturgical changes proposed, but on the whole question of authority within the church, and the rights of the bishops as opposed to central authority. The debate served both to hasten the emergence of progressist and curialist camps in the council — the use of Latin in the liturgy, and its biblical origins and significance being the chief lines of division — and to emphasize the parliamentary equality of the council fathers, irrespective of their position in the church.

The last point was important for the morale of the progressives. The curialists, having controlled the preparatory stages, had to some extent assumed the functions and privileges of ministers. Cardinal Ottaviani, in particular, was beginning to behave as though he were Floor-leader, or, in British parliamentary terms, Leader of the House, with the right to speak as often, and as long, as he wished, and to give the generality of the fathers unsolicited advice on how they should conduct themselves. His position as head of the Holy Office made him a formidable, and to some fearful, figure. He had been born in the poor quarter of Rome, the Trastevere, on the far side of the Tiber south of the Vatican, the son of a working baker (at the time, his brother still carried on the bakery), and had risen in the church by sheer hard work and an undoubted intelligence. His cheerfulness and wit won him friends even among his opponents, and his appalling eyesight aroused sympathy. Nevertheless, his apparent view that council regulations, while being strictly enforced against others, did not apply to himself, was bound to arouse antagonism. The cardinals who presided over the first days of the debates had rightly tried hard to enforce the ten-minute rule on speeches. Ottaviani had consistently ignored it, and had been allowed to do so. As the liturgical debate progressed, and more and more innovations anathema to him were freely proposed — communion in both kinds, concelebration, the use of the vernacular, the right of individual bishops to amend the liturgy to suit local conditions, and so forth — his authoritarian instincts rose to boiling point. On 30 October he intervened again, and asked: "Are these fathers plotting revolution?" Such changes would scandalize the faithful. They were supported only by a tiny minority (this was palpably untrue). Concelebration would turn the sacrifice of the mass into pure, or rather impure, theater. The liturgy was sacred ground: had not God warned Moses to remove his sandals when approaching the burning bush? Ottaviani went on and on; ten minutes passed; then fifteen. Cardinal Alfrink, presiding, at last interrupted: "Excuse me, Eminence, but you have already spoken for more than 15 minutes." Ottaviani, instead of leaving the rostrum, appealed to Archbishop Felici, the secretary general, another curialist. But Felici felt he could not bend the rules in such a flagrant fashion, and indicated to Ottaviani that he would have to surrender the microphone. As he did so, a round of applause — for Alfrink — burst from the body of the fathers. It was a humiliating moment for the man who had considered himself the most powerful official in the church, and he boycotted the council for the next two weeks.

Pope John's decision to have a fluid agenda proved a blessing in more ways than one, because it allowed the council to switch the subject when the debate on a particular schema began to flag. On 6 November, he ruled that when, in the view of the cardinal-presidents of the commission, the ground had been fully covered in debate, they could put a closure vote both on individual chapters within a schema and on a schema as a whole. This allowed the council to pass on from the liturgy schema (eventually carried by an overwhelming majority) to the debate on the "Sources of Revelation," which was introduced by Cardinal Ottaviani, who had now returned to his place, on 14 November.

Most of those present were aware that the *De Revelatione* issue would be the climax of the first session, and a real test of the balance of forces within the council and the church. The question at issue was simple and central to all others: were the doctrinal beliefs held and taught by the church based on the Bible, as it had been progressively interpreted by the tradition and authority of the church over many centuries? Or were there two distinct sources of divine revelation — the Bible, and tradition based on the church's authority? If the first, then there was no fundamental obstacle between the Catholic church and the other Christian churches. The progressive elaboration of doctrinal truth could proceed through biblical interpretation and exegesis. If the second, however, there was an insuperable obstacle, for the Vatican, as the custodian of the quite separate source of revelation, could proceed to interpret and elaborate doctrine as it thought fit.

The second, indeed, had been the position taken up by the church at the time of the Council of Trent and the Counter-Reformation. It had led, ultimately, to the First Vatican Council's decree of Papal Infallibility, and the subsequent use made of this dogma by the popes —

all of which had both widened the gap between the Catholics and other Christians, and had tended to increase the centralization of power in the pope and the Curia. In recent years, however, there had been a movement in the opposition direction. Progressive theologians taught that it was absurd to talk of two distinct sources of divine revelation: there was only one, the Bible as interpreted by a continuing tradition. The French Dominican Yves Congar put it neatly: "There is not a single dogma which the Church holds by Scripture *alone,* not a single dogma which it holds by tradition *alone.*" There was, of course, nothing essentially new in this position. In the earliest centuries of the church, the Bible had occupied precisely the central position to which the progressives now wanted it restored. Saint Athanasius himself had written: "The holy and divinely-inspired Scriptures are of themselves sufficient for the enunciation of truth." Saint Augustine had added: "In those things which are plainly laid down in Scripture, all things are found which embrace faith and morals."

Naturally, the restoration of the Bible to the central position in divine revelation would enhance the value and importance of biblical scholarship; and, indeed, the progressive theological movement in the church had been accompanied by a renaissance of biblical studies. Biblical exegesis had always been viewed by the Curia, and particularly the Holy Office, with intense suspicion. The one real complaint the curialists had against Pius XII was that, in his encyclical *Divino Afflante Spiritu* of 1943, he had appeared to open the floodgates to what they regarded as biblical adventurism, and the "corrective"

encyclical of 1950, *Humani Generis,* had, in their opinion, been inadequate to repair the damage. In the run up
to the council, therefore, they had been extremely active
in seeking to demolish positions of power held by the
Scripturalists. Their own fortress was the Lateran University, which they controlled, and they had been engaged on a systematic plan to centralize all teaching of
theology under its supervision. The one major university
outside their control was the Jesuit Biblical Institute of
Rome, of which Cardinal Bea had been for many years
the rector. In December 1960, the house journal of the
Lateran University, *Divinitas,* published a full-scale attack on the Institute, to prepare the ground for its sup-
pression or incorporation. It was written by Mgr. Antonio
Romeo, Cardinal Pizzardo's second-in-command at the
Congregation of Seminaries and Universities, which of
course is the Vatican ministry which supervises theological
teaching. An attack from such a quarter was a very serious
matter, and the congregation rubbed home the point by
sending copies to every bishop in Italy. What was more
reprehensible was that they altogether declined to publish a reply by the rector of the Institute. John was
shocked when a visiting Italian bishop commiserated
with him on the dreadful state of affairs at the Institute.
It was typical of John that he had not read the article,
and knew nothing about it: he always, if possible, tried to
steer clear of theological controversy — what the church
believed was always perfectly clear in his own mind —
and he was not in the habit of reading technical journals.
He called for the article, read it, and immediately sent
a message to the rector of the Institute assuring him of

his full confidence. What is more, he summoned Pizzardo and instructed him to write to Cardinal Bea, whose conduct of the Institute had naturally been part of the attack, assuring him that he, as head of the congregation, disclaimed any responsibility for the article. John was evidently very angry indeed. Nevertheless, the curialists persisted in their campaign. Early in 1961, the Holy Office informed the general of the Jesuits that two professors at the Institute, Stanislas Lyonet and Maximilian Zerwick, were suspected of teaching erroneous doctrine, and were to be removed. The general replied that he had personally examined their courses and found nothing amiss — where was the proof? In June, all the same, the Holy Office got the secretariat of state to intervene and suspend the two professors.

These incidents, and there were others, illustrate the problems John created for himself by his decision not to tackle the Curia or bring about wholesale changes in its personnel. His time was limited, and he did not believe in running his own intelligence service to discover what was going on. The curialists, on the other hand, were many, and they had all the time in the world to pursue their schemes, and to probe for new weaknesses in their opponents when one of their lines of attack was blocked. Nor were they inhibited by ordinary considerations of fair play or natural justice.

John, however, put his trust in the council, and it was justified. He knew that the schema on Revelation would reflect the views of the ultracurialists, and he thought this was no bad thing: let them be allowed to state their point of view openly, without qualification. He suspected they would overreach themselves, and they proceeded to do so. Some forewarning had been given by an article in the *Osservatore* published in June 1961. This had been written by Cardinal Ruffini, the archconservative, who had actually had the temerity to denounce the views on biblical studies expressed by Pius XII in *Divino Afflante Spiritu* as, quite simply, "absurd." The schema presented by Ottaviani on 14 November was a perfect digest of conservative and authoritarian attitudes. If it had been slightly more moderate in tone and content it might have raised serious problems for the progressives. As it was, it formed an easy target. It stated flatly that there were two sources of Divine Revelation. The Bible itself was not to be questioned: it repeated the statement in Leo XIII's encyclical, *Providentissimus Deus* (1893), that "the whole of Holy Scripture must be free from all error," thus repudiating all modern biblical scholarship. The Gospels were written by Matthew, Mark, Luke and John, and no one else. As for the Vulgate translation, it was free from error of any kind and could be quoted without possibility of mistake. The second source of revelation was tradition — "preserved in the church in continuous succession by the Holy Spirit [which] contains all those matters of faith or morals which the Apostles received either from the lips of Christ or at the suggestion of the Holy Spirit, and which they passed on, as it were, from hand to hand so that they might be transmitted by the teaching of the church." The schema, in effect, asked for a blank check for the *magisterium* of the church, investing it with a kind of secret body of Scripture to be expounded, as and when required, by the Vatican. In effect, it repeated the verdict of the Council of Trent at its fourth session, on 8 April 1546: nothing had changed in over 400 years. As Ottaviani himself added, in his introductory speech: "Our teaching is traditional, and will and must ever remain traditional." So the Curia was to be the ultimate custodian of truth.

When the debate was thrown open, the schema was immediately attacked, root and branch, by Cardinal Lienart, who was emerging as the chief spokesman of the progressives, and the head of a coalition of senior prelates from France, Germany, Austria, Holland and Belgium. "There are not," he said, "and never have been two *sources* of revelation. There is only one . . . the Word of God, the good news announced by the prophets and revealed by Christ. The word of God is the unique *source* of revelation." The lineup of speakers was predictable. Ruffini concluded: "This schema pleases me completely." Cardinal Siri, the young and highly conservative archbishop of Genoa, added that it was still necessary to support the condemnation of modernism of 1907. Opposed to the schema were, among many others, the cardinal-archbishops of Cologne, Vienna, Utrecht, Malines and Munich, Cardinal Léger of Montreal, and Cardinal Ritter of St. Louis, the outstanding American speaker at the council. Cardinal Bea pointed out that, among other things, the schema was totally lacking in pastoral spirit. The decisive speech, however, was made by Bishop de Smedt of Bruges. He spoke on behalf of the secretariat on Christian Unity, and, it was generally believed, on behalf of the pope himself. From the ecumenical point of view, he said, the schema was not only useless but actively harmful. There

were a number of rules which must be observed in opening a dialogue with other Christians, and all these had
been ignored. The advice of the secretariat had not been
sought by those who drew up the schema, and, when
volunteered, had been brushed aside. In the judgment of
the secretariat, the schema had "grave faults . . . it does
not represent progress but retreat." Unless it were modified, "we shall be responsible for causing Vatican Council
II to destroy a great, an immense hope. I speak of the
hope of those who, like Pope John XXIII, are waiting in
prayer and fasting for an important and significant step
to be made in the direction of fraternal unity, the unity
of those for whom Christ Our Lord offered this prayer,
Ut unum sint."

This speech, so clearly reflecting both John's thinking
and that of the majority of the council — it was greeted
with loud and prolonged applause — virtually clinched
the debate. The curialists had already begun to fall back
on procedural devices to protect their position. Ottaviani
had claimed, on 16 November, that the council's rules
did not provide for the rejection of the schema — an assertion promptly disproved by reference to Article 33.1
of the *Moto Proprio* governing procedure. He also denied
the assertion that the schema was the product of only one
school, the Lateran; but, as one cardinal said, "It is hardly
worth repeating that His Eminence is not telling the
truth. All the world knows it." After de Smedt's speech,
which Bishop Moorman called "perhaps the most important speech of the whole Council," and "the death-blow
to *De Fontibus Revelationis,*" there was no question that
a majority of the fathers wanted the schema withdrawn.

But what would be the size of the majority? On 20 November, the secretary, Felici, put the schema to the vote: those who wanted to halt the discussion were to vote "Yes," those who wished it to continue to vote "No." Putting the motion in this peculiar form led, as perhaps it was intended to lead, to great confusion. Many bishops voted "No" under the impression that they were voting against the schema, and thus found themselves in the curialist lobby. Even so, the progressives won by 1,368 to 822. But this was not a two-thirds majority, and the curialists therefore argued that the debate had to continue on the present schema.

The next day, after brooding over the position during the night, Pope John intervened. It was perfectly clear to him that an overwhelming majority of the fathers regarded the schema as hopeless, and wanted a new document to form the basis of discussion. A precedent had already been set for suspending the two-thirds rule, when he acted at the express wish of the council. Now he suspended it again and ordered the schema to be withdrawn. He took up a suggestion which had been made by Archbishop Garrone of Toulouse, that a new mixed commission be appointed to draw up a more acceptable schema. Bea and Ottaviani were to be joint presidents. Lienart and Meyer were to represent the liberals, Cardinals Browne and Ruffini the conservatives, and Cardinal Lefebvre of Bourges the center. The Theological Commission and the Unity Secretariat were to assist. The new schema, he added, was to be short, irenic in tone, and pastoral in approach. This was almost total victory for the progressives — indeed, when the schema finally emerged it was accepted by the council without fuss. What was remarkable about the crisis of 20–21 November, however, was that it revealed that a solid, and perhaps a very great, majority in the church were in favor of radical change, and that John was prepared to align himself with them. It was, as Henri Fesquet put it in *Le Monde,* "one of the great moments of the Council."

The debate on the Sources of Revelation set the tone for the rest of the first session. The schema on Christian Unity was overwhelmingly rejected, and the schema on the church came under heavy criticism, notably from Cardinal Montini, the future pope. The Curia was, in effect, told by the council, that, except on the liturgy, the preparatory work was wholly unsatisfactory, and that anything the council passed would have to be based on a genuine consensus. The council, in fact, had taken over, as John had hoped, and if the result, in the first session, appeared to be negative — a series of refusals — this was an indispensable preliminary to the constructive work which was to follow. That, at any rate, was John's view. He was delighted with the council's work. True, he had had to intervene twice; but on both occasions he had acted in accordance with the manifest desire of the majority; and, though he felt that the council should run its own affairs, he had always been prepared to give the ship a "touch on the tiller" if necessary.

John was not so much worried by the progress of the council as by a growing fear that he would not live to see its end, or even to continue to assist it during the second session, set for autumn 1963. In his journal he had complained of increasing physical discomfort as far back as

November 1961. Shortly before the council opened, he felt the first spasms of what was to prove cancer of the stomach. He had himself x-rayed, and the diagnosis of cancer was confirmed at the end of October, when the council was in midsession. The doctors described it to him as an ulcer, but both his confessor and his secretary thought it right to make it clear to him that his condition was serious. On the night of 26 November he had a hemorrhage and was in bed for several days. But by Sunday 2 December he felt well enough to appear at noon to give his usual blessing to the crowd in Saint Peter's Square. "Good health," he told them, "which threatened for a moment to absent itself, is now returning — has already returned." On Friday 7 December, the day before the council was due to disperse at the end of the session, he made his way into Saint Peter's on foot, recited the *Angelus,* and thanked the fathers for their work. The next day, the Feast of the Immaculate Conception, he attended a service of celebration and preached a short sermon. The first session had been "like a slow and solemn introduction to the great work of the Council." Lessons had been learned. The episcopal brethren had got to know each other. Of course there had been "sharply divergent views." But even this had "a providential place in the triumph of truth, for it has shown to all the world the holy liberty that the sons of God enjoy in the church." The council would go on: it would bring a "new Pentecost," a "clarion-call of God's kingship, of the brotherhood of men in charity, of the peace promised on earth to men of good will in accordance with God's good pleasure." The pope's voice was hesitant in tone when he began. But it gradually gathered strength. He was pleased to be in Saint Peter's, "the centre of Christianity," surrounded by such a great ecclesiastical gathering — which, as he now probably realized, he was seeing for the last time. He spoke of his "hour of heartfelt joy," and quoted Ecclesiasticus on the High Priest, Simon: "He himself stood by the altar and about him was the ring of his brethren." Then he gave the vast congregation his blessing, and walked slowly out of the basilica. It was the end of his contact with the council, but he still had important work to do in the last months which remained to him.

ELEVEN

The Quest for Convivienza

In November 1962, John XXIII celebrated his fourth anniversary as pope, his thirty-seventh as a bishop. He was eighty-one, and he knew he was soon to die. After his hemorrhage at the end of November, he made, on the whole, a remarkable recovery: not until his final illness the following May did he suffer another serious attack. He was often in fierce discomfort. On one occasion, when Monsignor Capovilla asked him how he was feeling, he replied: "Like St. Laurence on his gridiron." But he was able to carry on with his normal schedules of work; his last months as pope, indeed, were among his busiest. After the council dispersed early in December, however, he seems to have concluded that the affairs of the church were now in safe hands — the process of collegiality had been set in motion — and he could now concentrate his thoughts, in the short time left, on the state of the world. The image of peace, and the unity of mankind, became increasingly dear to him in his last period. It is notable, for instance, that his great encyclical *Pacem in Terris*, published at Easter 1963, was not addressed — as is customary — to the bishops and faithful but simply "to all men of goodwill." He saw himself less and less as the head of an ecclesiastical organization, more and more as a pastor to mankind.

There were occasional visits outside Rome, usually to parish churches which had caught his interest, because of some historical association, or because they housed the body of a saint he revered. Almost to the end he remained an indefatigable pilgrim. At the Vatican, he lived quietly with his small household staff — his secretary, his confessor, the four nuns from Bergamo who, under the direction of Mother Saveria Bertoli, did the cleaning and cooking, and his Venetian valet, Guido Gusso. After November 1962 his diet was very strict, and he took no wine (except on the occasion of Archbishop Slipyi's release), but it was offered to guests at his dinner parties, now increasingly rare. Often John would go to his tower. He had been a little taken aback at the extent and cost of the alterations which had been carried out to make it habitable for him, and in particular by the elevator which had been installed; now, however, he found it a boon. He liked to go to the roof, especially just before sunset. A group of German Catholics had presented him with a powerful pair of field glasses, and with these he would survey the magical skyline of Rome — its domes and cupolas, its arches, spires, pillars and pediments — and recite to himself, aloud, the names of all the churches he could identify. There, too, in fine weather, he would say

his evening rosary and read portions of the Office of the
Day.

There was an endless stream of visitors — heads of state,
prime ministers, musicians, authors, journalists. But, unlike Pius XII, John did not confine his private audiences
chiefly to celebrities; most of the time he was seeing visiting bishops, heads of religious houses, Vatican officials.
John was a businesslike pope even though, in an attempt
to cram everything into his schedule, he was nearly always
late for appointments. No one minded. John was worth
seeing when you got to him. Especially in his last months,
when he knew he was dying, he radiated a gentle humor
and a calmness for which the only word is beatific. Monsignor Capovilla has left a little pen portrait of him:

> He would always rise when a visitor came to see him. He
> tried to overcome the rigidity of protocol with the
> warmth of his gestures. Before he began a solemn act,
> there would always be a brief friendly word and look,
> as if to increase the "circulation" of understanding among
> his listeners. . . . His eyes would gently scrutinise but
> never intimidate. Whatever one said never seemed to up-
> set him. To someone in difficulty he would say: "I shall
> remember you in my rosary tonight, and tomorrow when
> I raise the chalice . . ." If he ever heard a bitter word, a
> look of bewilderment came over his face, like a child
> when he first hears a strange sound. Pope John would
> answer patiently then, trying not to shame but to miti-
> gate the impulsive anger he had been witness to.

John's visitors included, on many occasions, priests who
had come under attack from the Holy Office. If he was not
prepared to clash with the Curia head-on, he never hesi-

tated to protect its victims. Thus he curtly turned down Ottaviani's request that the Jesuit theologian, Karl Rahner, should be expelled from Rome, and he came to the rescue of the Dominican, Fr. Raimondo Spiazzi, who had had the temerity to publish a pamphlet which discussed a possible change in the church's insistence on sacerdotal celibacy. During this last period Pope John seems to have become increasingly disturbed by the obduracy of Cardinal Ottaviani: the persistence with which he pursued his opponents, his disregard of the pope's manifest wishes, his apparent lack of charity. A coldness, or rather a distance, grew up between them, though they were reconciled on John's deathbed.

John was concerned to protect communities, as well as individuals. One of the tasks he hoped the council would accomplish, even if he did not live to see it, was to issue a statement repudiating the collective accusations against the Jews, which the Catholic church had maintained over the centuries. John hated anti-Semitism, as he hated all racialism, and he believed that the church's teaching was partly responsible for it. In his first year as pope, he had marked Good Friday by saying mass at Santa Croce with a revised liturgy, in which the word *perfidis* (those without faith) was dropped from the prayer for the conversion of the Jews. He also rewrote a famous prayer of Leo XIII's to remove offensive references to Jews and Muslims. He was very anxious that the council should endorse his own attitude to the Jews in unmistakable fashion. After he died, at the second session of the council, Cardinal Bea introduced a statement on the Jews in the form of an appendix to Chapter Four in the document on ecumenism. This was described by Zachariah Schuster, European director of the American Jewish Committee, as "a total rejection of the myth of Jewish guilt for the Crucifixion." He said that the idea for the statement was John's own, but he had entrusted its actual phraseology to Cardinal Bea and his secretariat, who were asked to consult a wide range of Jewish and non-Jewish opinion before drawing it up. This was confirmed by Bea himself, on 19 November 1963. The previous December, he said, "I set out in writing for the Supreme Pontiff, Pope John XXIII of happy memory, a discussion of the whole question . . . after a few days the Holy Father indicated to me his full approval." Pope John obviously expected that the text he had approved would be accepted by the council unanimously and unaltered. Had he lived, there can be little doubt this would have happened. In the event, thanks to the irresolution of Pope Paul VI, the activities of the anti-Semites in the Curia, and the introduction of the quite irrelevant issue of Arab-Israeli politics, there was a battle over the text, which was substantially amended. The form in which it finally passed was perfectly satisfactory, but the long-drawn-out row destroyed the spontaneity and much of the significance of the gesture John had intended.

He was more fortunate in his relations with the Russians. John had extended feelers to Moscow almost from the first days of his pontificate (the details have not yet been disclosed), but there was little response until the Berlin crisis of August–September 1961. John put out a statement on 10 September which was deliberately universalist in tone. It appealed "to all our sons, to all those whom we feel the right and the duty to call such, to those who believe in God and his Christ, and also the unbelievers, because all belong to God and to Christ, by virtue of their origin and their redemption." The statement very much appealed to Khrushchev; it convinced him that here was a pope with whom he could do business. Ten days after it was issued, he gave an interview to Tass in which he responded warmly to the pope's appeal. This was the beginning of a curious relationship. As we have seen, Khrushchev gave qualified approval to the Ecumenical Council, made it possible for Iron Curtain clergy, and Orthodox observers, to attend, and personally arranged the release of Archbishop Slipyi. There was a further development in January 1963, when the official Soviet journal, *Science and Religion,* published an article on the council by its editor, Peter Kolonitski. Pope John's opening speech, he argued, had broken with the traditional anti-Communist policies of the Vatican, especially those of Pius XII. It was to be hoped this was evidence of a real change of heart. Even a religious event like the council was to be welcomed if it contributed to the chances of preserving peace. The reactionaries in the council, led by Ottaviani, were fighting hard to maintain the traditional political line of the church, and whip up anti-Socialist fervor. They might succeed. But the pope himself, and the majority of the council, favored the new line.

The article was one of a number which indicated that the Soviet press was taking a close interest in Catholic affairs. In due course, Khrushchev's son-in-law, Aleksei Adzhubei, then editor of *Izvestia,* made his appearance in Rome, and asked for an interview with John, which was granted on 7 March 1963. The interview itself was of no substance; it lasted only eighteen minutes, and was confined to courtesies and generalities. But it marked the first personal contact between the papacy and the Soviet establishment, and there can be little doubt that John hoped it would be followed, in due course, by a visit from Khrushchev himself. In an article published immediately after John's death, Bishop Cavagna, his confessor, wrote of John's constant attempts to improve his knowledge of languages. At the beginning of the pontificate, he said, John concentrated on English, as being most useful. During his last weeks, however, he was studying hard at Russian, "to show how much he loved that great people" — and, no doubt, to be able to greet the Soviet leader, when he appeared, in his own tongue.

In most of the world, John's international diplomacy was warmly supported. In Italy, however, it aroused bitter and outspoken anger on the right, both clerical and secular. John's rapprochement with the Soviet world moved forward *pari passu* with a changed attitude towards Italian politics. We have seen how faithfully John adhered, as patriarch of Venice, to Pius XII's rigidly anti-Communist and anti-Socialist electoral line. Even as pope, he took some time before carrying through a change of policy. Thus his earlier public statements on communism, from December 1958 to the summer of 1959, reflected the language and to some extent the spirit of Pius's admonitions. In April 1959 he seems to have made no attempt to stop curial officials or Italian bishops from endorsing the ban, issued by Pius, on Catholics voting for any Communist candidate, or any Socialist in electoral alliance with the Communist party. Two months later, on 3 July, a letter from Cardinal Pizzardo, then secretary to the Holy Office, to Cardinal Feltin, effectively ended the worker-priest movement. The campaign against the worker-priests had, of course, been launched many years before, and the destructive machinery had been set in motion before John's election. But he probably agreed with the decision: the same month he published his encyclical on the priesthood, *Sacerdoti Nostri Primordia,* which presents an idealized view of the calling, quite incompatible with factory labor. Thoroughout the first year of his pontificate, in fact, there was little to suggest he intended to take a radical political line. But his growing interest in international negotiations, his "bridge building" as he called it, convinced him that the church's traditional attitudes in Italian politics were obstacles to his diplomatic efforts. The truth is, he thought that politics were best left to laymen — it was part of his reverential approach to the priestly office. If a priest could not combine his vocation with factory work, was this not also true of politics? A cleric had no place on the hustings and no right to use his pulpit as an organ of propaganda. What was more, clerical attempts to influence voters were usually inept, and often counterproductive.

From the autumn of 1959, therefore, John gave increasingly clear indications that he did not wish the clergy to engage in Italian party politics. The matter came to a head in 1961–1962, when negotiations, ultimately successful, for a center-left coalition took place. This was a completely new departure in Italian postwar politics, since it involved the entry of the fundamentalist, or Nenni, Socialists into the government. The church had hitherto waged a bitter battle against Nenni candidates, since they usually operated an electoral pact with the Communists. John now let it be known that he did not wish the clergy, and especially bishops and senior Curia officials, to comment on the new coalition, one way or the other. They might not like it; or they might welcome it; in either case they were to keep their mouths shut. Again, this was not a command, but a clearly expressed wish. The great majority of the Italian clergy followed John's silent example. Almost alone, Ottaviani felt it necessary to express his hostility publicly. This time, Pope John found it necessary to administer a rebuke: cardinals, and the holders of great offices above all, had a duty to show their loyalty to the pope.

With the publication of *Pacem in Terris,* the church's attitude towards socialism, and indeed all Marxist-inspired political parties, changed fundamentally. Henceforth it became very difficult for any priests to assert, either in public or in the confessional, that a vote cast for a Socialist or Communist candidate was necessarily, and in all cases, sinful. The publication of the encyclical attracted enormous publicity, most of it not only favorable but enthusiastic. As with *Mater et Magistra,* John reinforced its success by ordering its widest possible distribution, and commanding bishops, heads of seminaries and other Catholic institutions, and the heads of religious orders, to ensure that it was read and studied. But there was resistance in some quarters. At the Italian elections of April 1963 the Christian Democrats lost ground, though they remained (as they still do) the dominant force in politics. The shift was predictable, and almost certainly the product of economic forces, but on the right Pope John was bitterly assailed as responsible for the lost votes: *Pacem in Terris,* the Adzhubei visit, his meddlesome negotiations with the Soviet Union, had combined, it was argued, to persuade many thousands of otherwise loyal Catholics to vote Communist or Socialist for the first time in their lives. These attacks hurt John, not least because he knew they were unjustified. But they did not deflect him from his policy. It was, to him, a simple matter of common sense that Catholics and Socialists should work together. And it was the will of Providence.

In any case, the critics formed only a small minority. After the successful opening of the council, the enormous publicity it had attracted now focused on Pope John himself. During his last months he became something like a world phenomenon, a man unique in his time. Unlike so many of his predecessors, he appeared not as a divisive, but a unifying, force in the Christian community; and, more than that, he represented to many believers of divers faiths, and to millions of men and women of no faith, the pure and elementary virtues of the religious disposition. In the aftermath of the Cuban missile crisis, as humanity realized how close it had come to the brink, Pope John seemed by the serenity and optimism of his words, a protective figure, a guarantee in his own calm and benignant person, that the world would not destroy itself, and that a mysterious Providence, as he said, was watching over the earth. *Pacem in Terris* was printed all over the world — sometimes in copious extracts, sometimes in full — in secular newspapers which normally gave only brief reports of papal encyclicals. It came at the right time; it struck the right note. It is not too much to say that, in conjunction with the lessons learned from Cuba, it helped to inaugurate the era of peaceful coexistence which, however uneasily, continues to our day. But John did not like the phrase "peaceful coexistence"; he thought it cold and inadequate. He preferred his own Italian word, *convivienza* — "living together."

On 1 March 1963, it was announced that the pope had been awarded the Balzan Peace Prize from a fund set up by Eugen Balzan, a self-made industrialist. The award committee was international, and included four Soviet representatives. John was told that his election had been unanimous, and the prize gave him great pleasure. He received it privately at the Vatican, but on May 10 he went to the Quirinale, the palace of the Italian presidency, to see the awards presented to the other Balzan recipients. It was, in its own way, a historic visit, for no pope had been to the Quirinale since the foundation of the Italian state, which the papacy had resisted so fiercely and so long. So the breach between the Italian nation and its predominant church was, to all appearances, finally healed. Much had been achieved since the days when young Father Roncalli had assisted Bishop Radini in his efforts to engage Catholics in the service of the state. It was historic in another sense: John's last public appearance. His pallor was deathly, and those who had not seen him recently were shocked by his evident physical weakness. But he contrived to read out a noble definition of his idea of peace: "Peace is a house, a house for everyone. It is the arc which unites earth and heaven, but to rise so high it has to stand on four solid pillars — truth, justice, charity and freedom."

John said his last Mass on 17 May, thereafter remaining, for the most part, in his bedroom, though on 20 May he came down to his library to receive Cardinal Wyszynski and a delegation of Polish bishops. He joked about his health and the likelihood of his survival until the second session of the council: "In September you'll either find me here, or another. You know, in one month they can do it all — the funeral of one pope, the election of another." That night he had another bout of bleeding, the first since November, which signaled the beginning of the end. His last weeks and days were punctuated by his sayings, as his staff and visitors remembered them. "When the body is afflicted, the soul has to adjust itself." "Every day is a good day to be born, and every day is a good day to die." Audiences were suspended from 22 May, but the following day, the feast of the Ascension, John appeared at his window to say the *Regina Coeli* with the crowd. He was aware not only that he was dying, but that his death might be prolonged and painful. He spoke of himself as "a victim of the altar, for the church, for the Ecumenical Council, and for the preservation of peace." He put out what was, in effect, a statement on his condition:

If God wants the sacrifice of the life of the Pope — that it may bring grace in plenty to the Ecumenical Council, to Holy Church, and to mankind which desires peace. If instead it pleases God to prolong this pontifical service — that it may be for the sanctification of the Pope's soul and of those who work and suffer with him to extend the kingdom of our Lord in Christian communities old and new, and in all the world.

He directed that those who were praying for him should keep these two alternative intentions in mind.

John had a remarkably strong constitution, and he did not die without a struggle. In the last few days of May there were relapses and recoveries. He summoned Cardinal Ottaviani, and embraced him. "See," he said, "we are about to enter the tabernacle of the Lord." There was no question of his faith: "I know in whom I have believed." John suffered much pain, not wholly alleviated by drugs. As befits a *bona mors* of the true Christian, he offered the pain as a sacrifice for his supreme intention, *Ut unam sint,* a phrase often on his lips during these last days. He said: "I have been able to follow my own death step by step, and now I'm going gently to my end." He heard the Pentecostal Mass lying in bed, and the following day, Whit Monday, 3 June, he was still alive, though occasionally relapsing into unconsciousness. These last few days there had been a continuous and vast crowd in Saint Peter's Square, as tens and even hundreds of thousands of Romans, and many thousands of visitors from all over the world, paid periodic visits to hear the latest news, and pray under the windows of the Vatican Palace. In the evening of 3 June, an open air mass was celebrated in the Square. Shortly after it was over, at ten to eight, Pope John died.

During the second session of the council, on 28 October — the anniversary of John's election — Pope Paul VI celebrated a special commemorative mass for him in Saint Peter's. The mass was a simple, dialogue mass, one of the earliest products of the council John had summoned, and it was the first time Pope Paul had conducted the ceremony in public. He was nervous, fumbled the opening prayers, and had to begin again. After the mass, Cardinal Suenens, one of the leading progressives at the council, went to the tribune and delivered an address on John's pontificate which summed up the feelings of those elements in the church which John had liberated and exalted. It was a remarkable oration, too long to quote in full. But one passage neatly portrays John's rare combination of spirituality and humanity:

> John XXIII was a man surprisingly natural and at the same time supernatural. Nature and grace produced in him a living unity, filled with charm and surprises. Everything about him sprang from a single source. . . . He was natural with such a supernatural spirit that no one detected a distinction between the two. Filling his lungs, as it were, he breathed the faith just as he breathed physical and moral health. He lived with the presence of God, with the simplicity of one who takes a walk through the streets of his native town. He lived with both feet on the ground, and with vibrant sympathy he was interested in the everyday concerns of people. . . . But he also lived completely in the world of the supernatural, in the familiar company of the angels and the saints . . . in him there was no dualism. His spontaneous, forthright, ever-alert goodness was like the sunshine which dispels fog and melts the ice, filtering through almost imperceptibly, like the most natural thing in the world, creating optimism along its path, spreading joy with its unexpected appearance, making light of all obstacles — not the sun

of the tropics, blinding with the intensity of its brilliance, but the humble, familiar, everyday sun, always there in its place, true to itself even when veiled by cloud — a sun we take for granted, so certain we are of its presence. He was not so naive as to believe that goodness will solve all problems, but he knew that it would open hearts to dialogue, to understanding and to mutual respect. He had confidence in the power of the charity of Christ burning in a human heart. . . . He will be for history the Pope of welcome and hope. This is the reason his gentle and holy memory will remain in benediction in the centuries to come. At his departure, he left men closer to God, and the world a better place for men to live.

Of course, history will deliver a less emotional and more prosaic verdict. History is concerned not merely with moments, and decades, of time but with the long-term consequences of actions which change their significance and value continuously as the years unfold. The ten years or more since Pope John died permit us to give only a provisional verdict on the effects of his pontificate which are still unveiling themselves in the work and structure of the Roman Catholic church, and its impact on the world. Not, perhaps, until the end of the century will it be possible to measure them in anything like a permanent perspective. But some tentative conclusions can be drawn.

John himself undoubtedly saw the Ecumenical Council as the central act of his papal ministry, and he was concerned not merely with what the council did but, even more so, with the manner in which it was done. He wanted to modernize and rationalize the decision-making processes of what had hitherto been an almost entirely authoritarian institution. This was the object of his doctrine of collegiality, and the council was his primary instrument for putting it into practice. The council, after four sessions, was brought to what many regarded as a triumphant conclusion: that is, the agenda was completed and many important changes introduced, usually by overwhelming majorities. Yet the end of the council left the more ambitious spirits in the church — those whom John had been most anxious to encourage — with a feeling of disappointment. John had regarded Cardinal Montini as his obvious, and perhaps natural and inevitable, successor. He had expressed his doubts about Montini: he was, he said, "Hamlet-like," inclined to agonize over decisions rather than move confidently forward in the trustful acceptance of the will of Providence. On the other hand, Montini had plainly and publicly identified himself with John's work; he was a man of immense experience and acknowledged ability, who had spent his life, as it were, preparing himself for high office in the church: he might be described as one born to be pope. John recognized in him experience and qualities which he himself lacked, and in particular the capacity to tackle the immense and detailed problem of the reform of the Curia. John was by temperament a pastor; as a central administrator he regarded himself as an amateur: it would, therefore, be right that he should be succeeded by one who could carry forward the movement with professional skill. This view was widely held, and it was reinforced when, immediately after John's death, and before the conclave met, Cardinal Montini preached a sermon indicating that there was no real alternative to the church but to pursue the initiatives John had taken. It would be too simple, and indeed unfair, to call this declaration an election manifesto: nevertheless, it was on the basis of this and similar statements that Montini emerged from the conclave as Pope Paul VI. Yet, as pope, Paul was never really at ease with the council John had summoned. Though he helped to push forward its detailed work, he was never able to accustom himself to the workings of collegiality. On two of the most contentious issues, artificial contraception and clerical celibacy, Paul abandoned the collegiate principle altogether, and took the decisions into his own hands.

It is hard to believe that John would have endorsed Paul's conduct. On both issues, John had been inclined to conservatism. But more important, to his mind, than his own personal views, or indeed to the intrinsic significance of the issues themselves, was the overriding principle that the council was the supreme legislative organ of the church. It was precisely because contraception and celibacy were contentious that the council was the proper forum for their discussion and resolution. John believed that, under Providence, the church could always reach a consensus: in the last resort, however acute the differences, however intractable the theological and disciplinary problems, Divine Wisdom would show the fathers a way, and the church as a whole would loyally follow. Mistakes had been made in the past, he thought, because successive popes had tried to resolve all the difficulties of the church in the solitude of their own minds: the council, and the collegiality it embodied, was to remove from the shoulders of the pope the immense burden of lonely decision. In these two cases, Pope Paul reverted to the earlier method; indeed, in the case of contraception he compounded his error by appointing an advisory commission of experts, and then rejecting its majority findings — thus underlining the personal nature of his decision. Since the pope, rather than the church, had decided that artificial contraception was unlawful, the verdict inevitably seemed to be provisional and temporal, valid only during the lifetime of the present incumbent of Saint Peter's chair. The result was that the pope's action, far from ending the controversy, merely pushed it into a new, and far more acrimonious, phase. Many priests openly refused to accept Paul's decision, and were disciplined, with varying degrees of success. Many others tacitly and privately opposed it; and their attitude was, in effect, endorsed by their superiors. Far more important, vast numbers of Catholic laymen and laywomen simply ignored the papal teaching. Respect for the person of the pope, which had stood so high under John, perceptibly declined, and the homogeneity of the church was eroded. Equally, Pope Paul's absolute insistence on clerical celibacy, without the sanction of the council, produced a crisis of conscience among many of the younger clergy, and large numbers resigned their orders rather than comply with a ruling which they felt to be lacking in conviction and natural justice. Morale among the clergy, which John's pontificate had so powerfully reinforced, was dramatically weakened. But transcending these two particular issues, however, was the confusion introduced by Paul's handling of them. John's aim, in reintroducing the conciliar system, had been to give the church a constitution, to place the administration of the canon law within, as it were, a parliamentary context. By emasculating the powers of the council, by introducing an arbitrary selection of "reserved matters" which the council was not authorized to handle, Pope Paul left unresolved the vital question of the ultimate origin of law. Did it lie in the pope himself, or in the Curia, or in the College of Bishops — that is, the universal church — or in a combination of all three? Or, alternatively, did each have authority in certain spheres, and, if so, which? These questions are still unanswered at the time of writing. And, until they are answered, and in a manner which the church as a whole can accept with good grace, this central aspect of Pope John's work will remain abortive.

Where Pope John's successor has pressed forward enthusiastically — some would say recklessly — has been in the reform of the liturgy. Vernacular services have been universally introduced. Latin has been largely, though not wholly, abandoned. The rigid form of the old Tridentine Mass, preserved unchanged for nearly four centuries, has been replaced by services which, it is argued, are much closer both to the spirit of the Christian sacrifice, and the practice of the early church. There have been wholesale changes in what might be termed the devotional machinery of Roman Catholicism: music and hymns, church furniture, rituals and pious practices, the liturgical calendar and the form and content of prayers. Many cherished early saints and martyrs, whose historical existence is dubious, have been consigned to oblivion; many quasi-superstitious cults have been discountenanced, or even banned. In general, the hieratic element in the church has been diminished, and the role of the congregation enlarged. Of course, in one sense this liturgical revolution embodies the spirit of *aggiornamento* Pope John conjured into existence. But it is doubtful whether its scope, and above all its pace, would have met with John's approval. He was conservative in such matters. More important, however, was his belief that the great mass of ordinary Catholics were conservative too, at least in the outward and visible practice of their religion. He thought that change should be radical in its essence, but he was wise enough to realize that change in the externals of devotion should be slow, deliberative and introduced on a basis of consent. If Pope Paul's decision on contraception provoked a crisis of conscience in the radical wing of the church, the ruthlessness of the liturgical changes has produced comparable strains at the other end of the spectrum of opinion. It could be argued, in fact, that Pope Paul contrived to get the worst of all possible worlds and on different issues alienated both progressives and conservatives, leaving the authority of the papacy on a very narrow basis of support in the center. In 1973, it was possible for a gifted Irish writer, Brian Moore, to publish a novel, *Catholics,* which is almost an ecclesiastical version of George Orwell's *Nineteen Eighty-four.* The novel, set in the non-too-distant future, concerns a papal emissary sent on a disciplinary mission to a remote island monastery off the West Coast of Ireland where conservative and recalcitrant monks are carrying on such forbidden practices as the Latin Mass and private confession — and, as a result, attracting enthusiastic pilgrims from all over the world.

The pace of liturgical change has, however, enormously strengthened the impetus of the ecumenical movement. In this respect Pope John's work has already achieved substantial results, with the promise of more to come. By changing the form, and to some extent the meaning, of the sacrifice of the mass, the Catholic church has drawn much closer, in fact and still more in spirit, to the "separated brethren." The doctrinal conflict between transubstantiation and consubstantiation, which played so baneful and bloody a role in the sixteenth century, has been placed in a new and sophisticated context, and is now plainly on the road to resolution. This is the first of the three great obstacles which bar the way to reunion between the Roman Catholic church, on the one hand, and the Anglican and Lutheran churches, and their offshoots, on the other. The second great obstacle — the validity of Anglican and similar orders, which Leo XIII had pronounced "utterly void" — has also been largely removed by the findings of the joint Anglican-Roman Catholic International Commission, whose report, *Ministry and Ordination,* was published at the end of 1973. The third obstacle, the authority and primacy of the papacy, is also being explored within the framework of the multitude of ecumenical contacts which Pope John established. The degree of authority of the papacy over the "separated brethren" is, of course, closely linked to the authority it possesses within the main body of the Catholic church, and it is unlikely that agreement can be reached until Pope John's principle of collegiality has been accepted by the Vatican in theory, and worked in practice: then, in the natural course of events, the separated episcopal churches will take their place in the collegiate machinery, and the problem of papal power will resolve itself. At the same time, the main Protestant churches themselves have been engaged in ecumenical negotiations with nonepiscopal Protestant denominations, so that it is possible to foresee, in the next decade or so, a general coming together of the Christian church on the basis of mutual tolerance, if not of absolute unity. Thus Christianity is steadily repairing the ravages wrought by the Reformation and the Wars of Religion, and this undoubtedly represents the fulfillment of what Pope John set out to achieve. By concentrating, as he constantly urged, on the points of agreement rather than the points in dispute, the progress made has been, by ecclesiastical standards, astonishingly swift.

In a wider sense, too, the teaching of Pope John has borne fruit. He wanted the church, and Christianity as a whole, to open itself to the world, to reintegrate itself with modern society. This was something, as he fully realized, which could not be introduced by papal *diktat,* but was a message to be conveyed and implemented by many thousands, indeed millions, of Christian priests and laymen. He wanted the sincere Christian to redefine his religious life: to see it not as a cult, to be ritually observed, in isolation from the rest of his existence, but as an all-pervading attitude of mind which embraced every aspect of human consciousness, and which linked him to every section of humanity, regardless of race or belief. This universalism was a projection of his own personal spirituality, at the center of which was a profound belief in the intimate unity of God and the creatures he had brought into existence. Naturally, it is impossible to quantify the extent to which this definition of the religious purpose has been accepted by the rank and file of the Christian communions. But certainly many Catholic priests and laymen now possess what might be termed an enlarged idea of the role of Christianity in the world, as a result of John's precept and example. They have left the condemned fortress of the elect and are mingling with mankind. The age of Catholic isolation is over, and in the long run this may prove to be Pope John's greatest legacy.

In the meantime, the world of the mid-1970s already looks a vastly different place to the one John left in summer 1963. It must be conceded that, to some extent at least, the mood of optimism which he both engendered and reflected in his church, and in society beyond, has disappeared. In secular affairs, Christianity, and Catholicism in particular, has failed to retain its position of centrality which, for a brief period, he secured for it. Violence in controversy, violence in fact, continue. Nor is this surprising. John was a man who furthered his aims by the projection of his personality, which was *sui generis*. He did not change structures, or lay down self-sustaining lines of action: rather, he established a mood in which, he believed, Providence could operate. To this extent he succeeded, but it would have been foolish to suppose that the mood would endure when his personality was withdrawn. The Roman Catholic church is a very ancient institution with a collective life of its own which survives the transient impact of its leaders, good or bad. And the world, too, is driven along by collective forces beyond the power of even the most striking of men to deflect substantially from their course.

The remarkable fact about Pope John is that he accomplished so much, some of it of permanent value. He breathed life into a church which was dying under the weight of its own monolithic structure. Since John, there has been no question of a return to the numb inanition of Pius XII's day: the pains it is now experiencing can be fairly described as symptoms of a return to sentient life. On a wider stage, John demonstrated that a spiritual leader, whose sincerity is self-evident, can still make the world pause and think, at least for a time. What more can fairly be demanded of a single individual, brought to prominence in the twilight of life and equipped with little more than a pulpit, albeit a global one? In this sense, his work and example are encouraging: the world is not so exclusively dominated by material forces as we are accustomed to suppose. But the life of a good man must be judged by its private as well as its public impact. John delivered his message of charity and hope not only to the collective multitudes but to many millions of individual human hearts, where it brought comfort and joy. He was a pastor, and that is how he will be remembered and revered, long after the times in which he lived have ceased to be relevant. There is a noble sentence in one of Francis Bacon's essays which could serve as John's epitaph: "Certainly, it is heaven upon earth, to have a man's mind move in charity, rest in Providence, and turn upon the poles of truth."

Select Bibliography

The Writings of Pope John

John wrote two biographical studies, *Il Cardinale Cesare Baronio* (new edition, Rome 1961), and his life of Bishop Radini, *Monsignor Giacomo Maria Radini Tedeschi* (new edition, Rome 1963, with additional material and notes, edited by Mgr. Loris Capovilla), and an edited selection of Saint Charles Borromeo's papers, *Atti della visita Apostolica di Santo Carlo Borromeo a Bergamo nel 1575* (Florence 1936–39); he also published a short study of early Italian seminaries, with special reference to Bergamo, *Gli Inizi del Seminario di Bergamo e Santo Carlo Borromeo* (Bergamo 1939). His writings on Catholic missions are collected in *La Propagazione della Fede* (Rome 1958). His official speeches and letters while nuncio in Paris are collected in *Mission to France* (trans. Dorothy M. White, London 1966). Some of his private letters are published, with notes by Monsignor Capovilla, in *Giovanni XXIII in alcuni scritti di Don Giuseppe de Luca* (Brescia 1963). His letters and speeches while patriarch of Venice are in *Scritti e Discorsi* (3 vols., Rome 1959). His "spiritual diary," that is, retreat notes, prayers, reflections, etc., from the age of fourteen, is published as *Journal of a Soul* (trans. Dorothy M. White, London 1965). His speeches and encyclicals as pope, and other relevant documents, can be found in the official *Acta Apostalicae Sedis* (Vols. L–LV, 1958–63).

Recommended for Further Reading

The best biographical account of John is Meriel Trevor: *Pope John* (London 1967); the best analysis of his policies as pope is E. E. Y. Hales: *Pope John and His Revolution* (London 1965). Translations of his major encyclicals are published by the National Catholic Welfare Conference (Washington, D. C.) and the Catholic Truth Society (London). Leone Algisi: *John XXIII* (trans. Peter Ryde, London 1963) gives an account of John's life up to his election as pope, and includes material supplied by John himself, who corrected the text before publication. Loris Capovilla: *The Heart and Mind of John XXIII* (trans. Patrick Riley, New York 1964) is an intimate study by his personal secretary; Henri Fesquet: *Wit and Wisdom of Good Pope John* (trans. Salvator Attanasio, New York 1964) is a collection of his sayings. For the Ecumenical Council, the best and most complete accounts are the four volumes by Xavier Rynne, *Letters from Vatican City, The Second Session, The Third Session* and *The Fourth Session* (London and New York, 1963–66). Useful background material and well-informed gossip are contained in Carlo Falconi: *Pope John and His Council* (trans. Muriel Grinrod, London 1964). Conciliar documents, with commentary, are published in *The Documents of Vatican II*, edited by Walter M. Abbott and the Very Reverend Mgr. Joseph Gallacher (London 1966). For a good, brief summary of the politics and work of the council, see George Bull: *Vatican Politics at the Second Vatican Council, 1962–5* (Oxford 1966). For the administrative structure of the Vatican, during and since the reign of Pope John, see Corrado Pallemberg: *Vatican Finances* (London 1971); Pallemberg's earlier work, *Vatican from Within* (London 1961) is also still useful, as is a more recent study, *The Politics of the Vatican* (London 1968) by Peter Nichols, correspondent of the London *Times*. For an American study of Pope John and the council see *Inside the Council* (New York 1963) by Robert Kaiser, correspondent for *Time*.

Other Works Consulted

Maria Luisa Ambrosini (with Mary Willis): *The Secret Archives of the Vatican* (London 1970).

Z. Aridi (with Michael Derrick and Douglas Woodruff): *John XXIII, Pope of the Council* (London 1961).

Ernesto Balducci: *John, the "Transitional Pope"* (trans. Dorothy M. White, London 1965).

Augustin Bea: *The Unity of Christians* (London 1963).

Christopher Butler: *The Theology of Vatican II* (London 1967).

Cuthbert Butler: *The Vatican Council, 1869–70* (revised ed., London 1962).

J-Y Calvez: *Église et Société Économique* (2 vols., Paris 1959).

R. Caporale: *Vatician II: The Last of the Councils* (Baltimore 1964).

Louis Chaigne: *Portrait de Jean XXIII* (Paris 1964).

John G. Clancy: *Apostle for Our Time: Pope Paul VI* (London 1964).

Yves Congar: *Report from Rome: The First Session of the Vatican Council* (London 1963).

Davide Cugini: *Papa Giovanni, nei suoi primi passi a Sotto il Monte* (Bergamo 1965).

Louis Dupré: *Contraception and Catholics: A New Appraisal* (New York 1964).

Carlo Falconi: *Il Silencio di Pio XII* (Milan 1965).

Michael Fogarty: *Christian Democracy in Western Europe, 1820–1953* (London 1957).

R. Fontenella: *Pope Pius XI* (trans. M. E. Fowler, London 1938).

Anne Freemantle: *The Papal Encyclicals in Their Historical Context* (New York 1963).

Saul Friedlander: *Pius XII and the Third Reich* (trans. Charles Fullman, London 1966).

Hieronymo Dal Gal: *Pius X* (trans. T. F. Murray, Dublin 1954).

Oscar Halecki: *Pius XII* (London 1954).

E. E. Y. Hales: *Pio Nono* (London 1960).

Hubert Jedin: *Storia del Concilio di Trento* (2 vols., Brescia 1949).

Hans Kung: *The Structure of the Church* (London 1964).

Andrea Lazzarini: *Giovanni XXIII* (Rome 1958).

John Moorman: *Vatican Observed* (London 1967).

Guenter Lewy: *The Catholic Church and Nazi Germany* (New York 1964).

E. J. Mahoney: *Questions and Answers* (2 vols., London 1949).

John McKenzie: *Authority in the Church* (London 1966).

Jacques Nobecourt: *Le Vicaire et l'Histoire* (Paris 1964).

Michael Novak: *The Open Church* (London 1964).

Walter H. Peters: *Benedict XV* (Milwaukee 1959).

Leo Pyle (ed.): *Pope and Pill* (London 1968).

Norman St. John-Stevas: *The Agonising Choice: Birth Control, Religion and the Law* (London 1971).

E. H. Schillebeeckx: *Vatican II: The Struggle of Minds* (London 1963).

George Siefer: *The Church and Industrial Society* (London 1964).

E. Soderini: *Leo XIII* (2 vols., trans. Barbara Carter, London 1934).

Léon Joseph Suenens: *Co-responsibility in the Church* (London 1968).

Domenico Tardini: *Pius XII* (Vatican 1960).

Bernard and Barbara Wall: *Thaw at the Vatican* (London 1964).

R. Webster: *Christian Democracy in Italy, 1860–1960* (London 1961).

A. Wenger: *Vatican II, Première Session* (Paris 1963).

Index

AFG7722-1